PATHWAYS TO MASTERY

BY SCOTT ALLAN

THE SERIES

scottallan@scottallanpublishing.com

Empower Your Best Habits

*Optimize Your Performance and Cultivate Better
Habits in Your Life, Work, and Relationships*

Pathways to Mastery Series

Master Your Life *One Book at a Time*

*Available where **eBooks, books** and Audiobooks are sold.*

Empower Your Best Habits

Optimize Your Performance and Cultivate Better Habits in Your Life, Work, and Relationships

By Scott Allan

Scott Allan
PUBLISHING
ONE BOOK AT A TIME

S A

ISBN (Paperback): 978-1-990484-30-8
ISBN (eBook): 978-1-990484-28-5
ISBN (Hardcover): 978-1-990484-29-2

CONTENTS

JOIN THE COMMUNITY OF 30,000 LIFETIME LEARNERS!

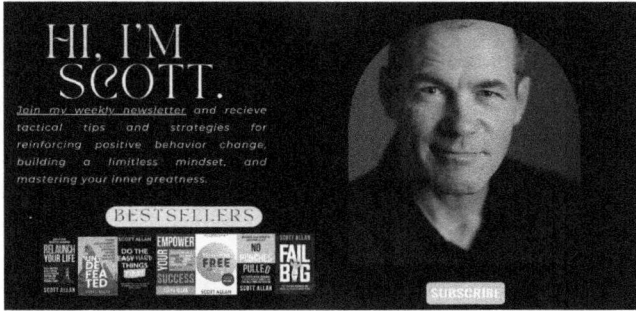

Sign up today for my **free weekly newsletter** and receive instant access to **the <u>onboarding subscriber pack</u>** that includes:

The Fearless Confidence Action Guide: 9 Action Plans for Building Limitless Confidence and Achieving Sustainable Results!

The bestseller poster pack: A poster set of Scott Allan's bestselling books

The Zero Procrastination Blueprint: A Step-by-Step Blueprint to Turn Procrastination into Rapid Action Implementation!

Begin Your Journey and Make This Life Your Own.
Click Here to <u>Subscribe Today</u>, or scan the <u>QR code</u> below.

"All big things come from small beginnings. The seed of every habit is a single, tiny decision."

— **James Clear**, bestselling author of *Atomic Habits*

Introduction: Empower Your Best Habits

"And once you understand that habits can change, you have the freedom and the responsibility to remake them."

—**Charles Duhigg**, *The Power of Habit*

We aspire for many things in life. We all set different goals and desire to achieve specific goals related to health, wealth, professional success, financial stability, relationships, love life, abundance, spirituality, fitness, nutrition, and anything else.

While in this pursuit, sometimes we fall short of actualizing our goals, and sometimes, we emerge the other end victorious.

Why do we succeed in certain ventures and enjoy specific results but fail in others? Some may think the answer is excellent time management, self-discipline, or strong willpower. Others may have different answers.

For a moment, assess these qualities and virtues.

What does time management center around? It's all about creating schedules, differentiating high-priority tasks from low-priority ones, sticking to your plan, doing things timely, and avoiding time wasters, right? Of course, you could add more practices to the list, but this rough list covers everything about effective time management.

Similarly, if you analyze self-discipline, you will realize that it is about sticking to what's essential, saying no to unnecessary stuff, and convincing yourself to stay on the right track.

Every successful habit boils down to certain practices done consistently and habitually. You may vow to stay hydrated, but if you drink 3 liters of water one day and go back to your old routine of drinking barely three glasses a day, your hydration levels will stay poor. To achieve any goal, you must build the proper HABITS that yield that same result.

I'll now go back to the question I asked above: *What makes us succeed in certain ventures and enjoy specific results but fail miserably in others?*

The response is that **your daily habits lead the way regarding your performance level in growth and potential.**

For this reason, Aristotle articulated that man is a creature of habits. Your life is a product of all your positive, negative, or neutral habits. Your habits unequivocally shape your life. Yes, this does mean that if you wish to become healthy, happy, prosperous, spiritual, confident, wealthy, and productive, you need to work on building habits conducive to these particular results.

How can you figure out those habits and train yourself to build them? We have got you covered in that regard.

Empower Your Best Habits is a complete blueprint for understanding the significance of habits in your life. Now you will learn the tactics and strategies for building success, sustainable wealth, and long-term happiness, while experiencing a new level of health and spirituality.

I am confident, proactive, peaceful, healthy, and wealthy, and living an abundant life characterized by joy, tranquility, and meaning. All this is possible only due to the great habits I have built. I sincerely want you to achieve the same and even more.

Whatever I have achieved in life is because of the brilliant, powerful habits I have forged over time, and if I can do it, I believe anyone is capable of doing the same.

With this book, I promise that you will receive the knowledge, power, and strategies to transform your habits and life for the very best. Here's what **Empower Your Habits** will educate you on and what it can do for you:

- The science behind habit formation—which will help you understand how habits work

- Understanding the habit loop— to ensure you can comprehend its elements

- The strategies to build good habits and break bad ones

- The art of developing a sticky habit

- Debunking popular habit-related myths

- Powerful productivity habits that can skyrocket your productivity

- Best wealth habits to help you achieve financial abundance and prosperity

- Best practices for successful people to boost your willpower and build self-discipline

- Some of the best mental practices to create a growth and wealthy mindset

- Spirituality habits so you figure out a clear sense of direction in your life and achieve your purpose

- Best practices for good health to improve your physical, mental, and emotional health

As you read this book, you will figure out new ways to live your life in the most meaningful manner and become the greatest version of yourself.

Besides getting actionable and potent information to sculpt your best life to date, you will also get the ease of doing it at your pace, according to your convenience, based on the outcomes you want on a priority basis in your life.

Empower Your Best Habits is a little different than the rote self-help books on habits in the market. It does not require you to read the book from start to finish to understand it, nor does it demand that you have a clear understanding of the first chapter to understand the last one.

How to Read Empower Your Best Habits

I've divided this book into different parts, with each of those parts segregated into different chapters. The first chapter of the first part will focus solely on habit formation and the ins and outs relevant to the subject. It will help you understand the subject at a level that will allow you to build or break any habit you want.

After that, every part of the book will center around a particular aspect of your life and the outcome you would want to achieve in that key area. Each part contains different chapters, each of which talks about the different mini habits you can build, including a step-by-step process detailing how to build those habits to accomplish your goal.

For example, in the section on 'Productivity Habits,' we will talk about the various habits you must build to boost your productivity and workflow efficiency.

In this book, you will find the best habits to adopt and practice in the following aspects:

- Productivity/Workflow Habits

- Health

- Wealth Habits

- Wellness and Thinking

- Mindset Habits

- Personal Growth Habits

- Time Management Habits

- Spirituality Habits

This segmentation of different habits in different areas of your life is what makes this book an easy read. You can start the book from any part or page and learn something incredibly powerful.

If you are struggling with your personal growth, jump to the chapter detailing habits on personal growth. If you want to know how to increase your wealth, move right to that particular part.

You need not peruse through every habit in every part: you can skim through the entire part and every chapter or jump right into a particular habit related to an outcome you want. If your time management skills are not too questionable, and you only sometimes battle with discerning between high and low priority tasks, you can focus on that habit.

You don't have to stick to any pattern or schedule to read this book. It is an easy-to-read-and-understand guide meant to help you build the best habits for success that flows together very smoothly.

The book will make perfect sense irrespective of whether you read the entire book in a chapter-by-chapter manner or peruse through any particular chapter in any part of the book. It is as simple as that.

Let us kick start this journey that will move you towards your dream life...a life of developing good habits toward success.

"Feeling sorry for yourself, and your present condition is not only a waste of energy but the worst habit you could possibly have."

— **Dale Carnegie**, *How to Win Friends and Influence People*

Part 1: The Science of Habit Formation

"Wouldn't it be great to be gifted? In fact... It turns out that choices lead to habits. Habits become talents. Talents are labeled gifts. You're not born this way, you get this way."

— **Seth Godin**

Chapter 1: How to Develop a Habit

"There is no influence like the influence of habit."
— **Gilbert Parker**

Your habits influence how you think, behave, act, and decide different things in life. They are crucial to the quality of your lifestyle and overall well-being. This is why it is essential to know how to develop good habits in alignment with your desired lifestyle and goals because, only by building the right habits can you live a joyful, prosperous, and fulfilling life.

What is Habit Formation?

All of your behaviors become patterns. You do not think twice before performing most of your actions. That is how a habit forms and patterns are established.

The process through which a certain behavior becomes permanent and automatic in your life is called 'habit formation.' You can form a habit unconsciously without consciously intending to develop it, but you can also deliberately cultivate it. When a specific behavior shifts to autopilot mode, it becomes your habit because it does not demand conscious attention.

Some people also confuse a routine with a habit. A routine involves repeated behavior, but it may or may not be in response to a deep-seated impulse, as in the case of a habit. A habit is strongly associated with an impulse or an urge to do something. If you wash the dishes just because they are dirty, and it's a chore you must do without feeling a powerful sense of craving, it is a routine, not a habit.

The 'Habit Loop' and 'Habit Formation' Comparison

Two terms often discussed regarding habits are habit formation and habit loop. Let's distinguish between the two.

Habit formation is the entire process through which a behavior—or an act—goes through different rounds in your life and then attains a permanent status. On the other hand, a habit loop is a cycle that contains the components involved in forming a habit. When repeated over time, the elements in a habit loop form a habit. Hence, a habit loop is a cycle that, when played continuously, leads to habit formation.

The following are the components of the habit loop:

Reminder/Trigger/Cue: This is what triggers the onset of a habit and reminds you to engage in it. It can be an object, time, place, feeling, person, event, or even an amalgamation of a couple of these factors.

The reminder tells your brain to move into autopilot mode and which habit to pull out to engage in. If you have a habit of sleeping at 9 PM, you will start feeling drowsy closer to 9 Pm. In this case, time is the habit's reminder.

Routine/ Behavior: This refers to how you engage in a particular habit. It can be emotional, physical, or a combination of the two. If you go for a 10-minute stroll in your garden while humming a tune before every meal, that's the routine for your pre-meal walk habit.

Reward: This is the outcome of engaging in a particular habit. Just as humans are social creatures, they are also somewhat greedy creatures. We only engage in behaviors regularly when they promise us some outcome in return.

Every habit, be it a good, bad, or neutral habit, has one or more associated rewards. The reward associated with a pattern helps your brain determine if that particular loop is worth keeping in the long run. For example, you brush your teeth twice daily to maintain oral hygiene and steer clear of dental problems. You may smoke because it relieves stress.

Since the three components start with an R: reminder, routine, and reward, these three are also known as the *3Rs of Habit Change*. This entire loop relevant to a particular habit becomes more automatic with time.

The reminder and reward become intertwined to a point where you start experiencing a strong sense of craving and anticipation for the habit. The 3 R's are integral to making and breaking habits; we'll discuss why in the following chapters.

The Science Behind Habit Formation

The brain carries out a process known as 'chunking,' which converts a series of actions into a programmed routine. Chunking lays down the foundations for habit formation.

According to scientists, we build habits because the human brain is always fishing for new ways to save more time, effort, and energy. The brain tries to turn any routine into a consistent habit. When you form a habit, you don't have to overthink about acting a certain way or doing things in a specific manner. Since the thinking time gets shortened, the effort to gets minimized.

The first time you made yourself poached eggs and tea, you would have taken quite a while. You had to make sure to break the eggs in a colander and were probably extra careful when brewing the tea. Two years down the road, you probably make the same breakfast in a jiff, and near-perfectly every time; the activity has become an automatic routine and does not feel like a burden to you anymore.

Habits help you save effort. With more behaviors on autopilot, your brain becomes efficient. You start doing things faster, get more results, and move closer to your targets in less time. However, this does not mean that your brain stops working or that your brain wants to develop habits to lessen its burden. With a behavior on an automatic loop, your brain does not need to actively and fully participate in decision-making. It can then divert its attention to other activities and stop working hard.

The 'sticky habit' technique is a great approach to help develop habits.

How to Build Sticky Habits

As suggested by the name, a sticky habit is a habit that sticks around for a long time, even years after its formation. It sticks to another habit, and that habit works as a trigger for the new, sticky habit.

To build a sticky habit, you need to figure out the habits you want to stick to and those you want to unstick. To practice this approach, you need to follow four primary steps:

First, you need to figure out the habit you want to stick around and stay disciplined with it for about 60 days. To ensure one habit acts as the trigger for another, you must figure out what other pattern to stick this new one onto.

Next, you need to reward yourself for sticking to this habit to stimulate the release of dopamine and serotonin, thus ensuring you stay committed to it.

Now, nourish and train your brain every day to make it easy to work on the respective habits.

Finally, set reminders to stay consistent with the sticky habit.

In its most basic sense, the sticky habit approach is about building a reward system that links the reward to the action. You also need to change your perspective on bad habits because only by understanding how destructive they are can you let them go and build something new.

After this introduction, you now have a better understanding of how habits work and how you build them over time. Let us now move to the next chapter of this part of the book and understand how to make good habits and let go of bad ones.

Chapter 2: How to Break Bad Habits

"A habit cannot be tossed out the window; it must be coaxed down the stairs a step at a time."
— *Mark Twain*

The habit change process isn't complicated or challenging. It is, however, one that demands consciousness and thoughtfulness. People often struggle with breaking bad habits and bringing positive ones in their place due to faulty approaches. Let's resolve this problem in this chapter.

You Cannot Break a Bad Habit.

Is this true? Can you not break a bad habit?

Well, the simple fact is, you cannot break a bad habit, at least not entirely.

That does not mean you cannot replace it. The reality is that you cannot eliminate a bad habit; you have to **replace it.** A bad habit is also very sticky, but even though you can replace it, the memory of your bad habit sticks around until you need it again.

Every habit you have, good or bad, exists in your life for a reason. All your habits, even the bad ones, benefit you in one way or another. At times, as in the case of drug abuse, smoking, or alcoholism, the reward is biological. Sometimes, the reward is emotional, as is the case of being in a toxic relationship. In other cases, bad habits, such as pulling your hair, biting your nails, or clenching your jaw are coping mechanisms we use to handle stress.

All these benefits extend to smaller bad habits, too. The practice of checking your text messages every time you pick up your phone may make you feel connected to the world around you. Simultaneously, checking those emails ruins your focus, productivity, and peace of mind. However, if you don't do that, you get an intense wave of FOMO (fear of missing out), so you engage in that practice repeatedly.

Since bad habits come with some benefits or obvious perks, it is not easy to ditch them, which explains why when someone asks you to 'just stop smoking' or 'stop being lazy' or 'stop eating junk food,' you cannot just do it.

The good news is that there is a way through this challenge. Instead of breaking a bad habit, focus on replacing it with another habit.

The Key to Breaking Bad Habits

Naturally, something that has developed over time won't be easy to let go of. You have to be tactful in detaching yourself from it; this is where **habit replacement** comes into play.

A bad habit leaves when you find a substitute for it. This time around, however, you need to make a very mindful and deliberate decision. You have to pay attention to bringing in a habit that has the following two characteristics:

Yields the same, similar, or even better reward as the bad habit you wish to change: We only build habits that bring us some rewards. To kick out a bad habit from your life for good, you need a replacement that makes you feel the same way.

With that bad habit gone out of your life, you will crave it. Say you decide to stop smoking. Every time that you are not smoking, especially when you experience the trigger for the habit of smoking, you will get a strong urge to smoke. You will miss the feeling brought on by holding a cigarette.

Importantly, you will miss the rewarding feeling of stress relief— or whatever you sought from smoking. That feeling will compel you to resume smoking, causing you to rebound.

To ensure that does not happen, you have to bring in something that gives you the same feeling and results, or better, even more excellent results. That rewarding feeling fills in the void left by the bad habit.

Produces robust, positive effects on your personality and life: It is important to seek a habit with positive effects that nullify the toxicity left in your life by the bad habit you have just broken. The rewarding feeling associated with the bad habit consumes you and clouds your ability to think rationally.

You start to enjoy the bad habit irrespective of its adverse effects. For example, we know that smoking damages the lungs weakens the immune system, and increases the risk of cardiovascular diseases. Despite being aware of the harmful consequences of smoking, the relaxation it offers—and its other rewards—compels you to stick to the practice.

You allow it to deteriorate your health courtesy of that rewarding feeling. But a happy and thriving life does not come at the cost of your health; never forget that.

To build your best life to date, you must empower yourself with good habits that yield positive results. Thus, when looking for a substitute for a bad habit you want to let go of, search for something beneficial.

With that settled, let us discuss the **step-by-step process of breaking a bad habit**.

The Step-By-Step Process to Replace Bad Habits

Here's how you can replace bad habits with more effective and intentional practices that help you build the life of your dreams:

Figure out the habit you need to replace.

Analyze how it affects your life and determine why you need to change that habit. For example, if you wish to change your smoking habit, contemplate why you must let go of it. These reasons are your compelling whys that strengthen your willpower, motivating you to stay strong when you feel sidetracked.

Observe the habit in detail for some time paying close attention to its cues, routine, and reward. Doing this gives insight into what triggers the practice, allowing you to start avoiding and better managing those reminders and routines, further enabling you to know how you carry out that behavior and the rewards, which helps you to understand what motivates you to stick to that behavior.

Once you become aware of the triggers, **develop a tighter grip** on managing them. Start avoiding people, places, and things that remind you of the bad habit under review. Also, build an environment that diverts your attention away from those triggers.

At the same time, **make a list** of specific practices that promise the same or similar reward as the bad habit under question. Try each of those, one at a time, assess the reward and outcomes they result in and see if they work in steering you away from the bad habit.

Frequently **work on the practices** you enjoy the most and those that effectively divert your mind off the bad habit.

Take some time **experimenting with different activities** and behaviors, and soon you will find an excellent alternative to that unhealthy habit you wish to change.

Give yourself around **66 to 90 days to build the habit** for sustainability. It usually takes a habit this time duration (sometimes even more) to stick around. But this also means you must continue the habit to keep it active.

When you engage in a particular habit in place of a bad habit, carry it for the entire length of the bad habit's routine. For example, if you smoked two cigarettes in a row for about 15 minutes and are trying to replace it with meditation to stay calm, **meditate for 15 minutes**.

Another way to go about this is to have a **couple of practices stacked upon one another** for that period. Also known as habit stacking, this approach engages you in meaningful activities, one on top of another, distracting you from the bad habit.

Reward yourself with a personal gift or treat once you constantly work on building a good habit for a consistent period.

Start working on these guidelines, and soon enough, you will have a new and healthy habit in place of the bad one you wanted to eliminate.

You can build a good habit in the same manner too. That said, making a good habit and ensuring it stays permanent in your life requires more effort and a slightly different strategic approach.

Chapter 3: How to Build a Sustainable Sticky Habit

"Positivity is like a muscle: keep exercising it, and it becomes a habit." — **Natalie Massenet**

Just like a muscle grows bigger and stronger with proper exercise, the continual practice of a specific action turns this action into a habit when you work on it consistently. This is the key to habit building—taking action with the intent to develop a new skill. After discussing how to improve bad habits, let us develop good ones.

First, it is essential to understand the need to build good habits.

The Need for Good Habits

Why do you brush your hair before going to work? The obvious answer is that it makes you look presentable.

Now let me ask you another question: if you have a habit of working out regularly, why do you do it? It's most likely because it gives you a more robust and leaner body and keeps you physically and mentally fit.

Both the practices I mentioned above have one or more positive effects on your life, and that's why you continue to perform them daily. Like bad habits, good habits also have rewards—usually better ones. They add convenience, value, structure, joy, productivity, quality, and abundance to your lifestyle.

All of us want to be and live a certain way. Some of us aspire to fitter bodies; others may want to be more prosperous. Some may want to be more disciplined at work, while others want to experience more profound peace of mind.

Everything we wish for can be ours only if we build the proper habits targeted toward those outcomes. That is the power of positive habits: *they take you closer to your desired reality and help you live a more meaningful life.*

How to Build Good Habits

Good habits infuse a lot of productivity, fulfillment, and energy into our lives. Here's how you can create these powerful effects through habit formation.

Think of the result or impact you want to experience in your life. Do you want to become healthier, wealthier, happier, more productive, spiritual, or successful in your business?

It is crucial to **determine the exact outcome** you want; Only then can you identify the proper habits to build in order toto achieve the desired result.

Once you have determined the desired result, **decide on the habit you wish to build**. If you want to be healthy and physically fit, do you want to work out daily, or do you want to start eating fresh fruits regularly? If high productivity is what you are looking for, do you want to write 3,000 words daily for your book?

Sometimes, figuring out the exact habit you need to develop to achieve the anticipated outcome can be difficult. In that case, you can **find a couple of practices you need to build**. For instance, to be healthy, you can create the habits of exercising, drinking more water, sleeping well, and eating a healthy diet.

However, it is best to **begin with one habit at a time** because it makes it easier to adjust to the new routine you are trying to bring into your life.

Think of **that habit** and why you must incorporate it into your life. Reflect on its meaning in your life and the rewards it brings forth. If you want to exercise daily, list the physical, mental, and emotional health benefits of working out. The benefits are what you are trying to achieve and the compelling whys that will make you stick to the habit change process.

Remember, no goal is easy or difficult to achieve. Everything is easy if you put your mind and heart into it, and even the most straightforward things become monstrous if you don't build exemplary commitment.

However, there are phases in your life when your motivation runs low and your willpower gets depleted. You become exhausted, lose track of your whys, get distracted, or go through any other struggle that makes you stray from your habit change process.

During these times, you must **revisit your compelling why** to rediscover why you started in the first place. When you do, your motivation slowly gets back on track, and you are sailing the 'habit change' voyage again. I recommend you write **down your compelling why** and go through this at least twice daily to clarify why you will work on this mission.

Next, **figure out the routine you will be building.** If you plan to exercise, for how long will you exercise? What exercises will you do? Are you going to do more cardio? If you are doing leg lunges or squats, how many reps in a set, and how many sets in total?

Similarly, if you plan to drink more water, how many liters of water are you looking to consume? If it is 3 liters/day, how many glasses will you drink after a certain period? Figuring out the routine helps you know how to carry out the practice, what goes into it, and how long you have to work on it.

Such distinctions give you clear instructions to work on it, simplify the process, and remove any ambiguity you may have. Create the habit breakdown and analyze it several times to clear out any lingering confusion.

Think of when you would like to begin the habit change and possibly the time you need to turn it into something permanent. For instance, if you want to exercise daily, think of **when you would like to begin**: next week or the week after that?

Also, **think of the goal you want to achieve**. For example, if losing weight is the intention behind your desire to exercise, what is your weight loss target, and how long will it take you to accomplish it? If you are trying to lose 40 pounds, will it take 5 or 6 months to achieve it? Keep in mind the pace at which you work, your current routine, and how easy or hard it will be for you to work on the habit change.

Perhaps, you plan to work out for 10 minutes only at the start for about three weeks and then slowly increase your workout duration while trying to eat healthily. In that case, it can take you more than six months to lose 40 pounds, and that's perfectly fine. **Understand your pace** and **adjust the timeline** accordingly. Through this process, you can build a workable routine.

Write down the goal you wish to actualize and **the habit change you want to bring about** in your journal and create an intention around it. If you're going to write daily so you can publish an e-book, write down, "I will write 3,000 words daily to publish my book by the end of December 2022." Chant these words ten times to embed the suggestion in your mind. Once your subconscious accepts it, it makes you work accordingly towards achieving the desired result.

Next, tweak the suggestion into a more affirmative and present-oriented indication. An affirmative commitment suggests you are doing something, and a present-oriented promise makes you feel you are taking action at the moment to objectify your goal.

When your mind accepts that you are working on a particular goal, it constantly keeps you focused on it. In this manner, you concentrate your efforts and energies on the desired habit change and keep working in the right direction that eventually takes you towards your goal.

Once you have created the entire plan, write down your milestones spread over a specific time duration. Write down your targets to ensure you can measure your performance at regular intervals and track your progress towards the goal. For example, if you want to lose 40 pounds in 5 months, how much do you propose to lose monthly?

What's the next step? Start working on it! Work on it regularly, keep powering through, and measure your results.

Keep yourself motivated by setting enticing rewards to enjoy at every milestone. On losing 5 pounds, you can go to a movie; on shedding 15 pounds, you can buy yourself a nice dress/shirt you have been eyeing for a while; and on achieving your final target of melting away 40 pounds, you can take a little weekend getaway with your partner.

Rewards incentivize you to achieve what you want and keep your interest and enthusiasm alive as you move swiftly and work towards what you want to achieve.

To keep working on the preferred habit change with high octane energy, you need to understand the relationship between willpower and habits; after all, you will need lots of willpower to accomplish your target.

Chapter 4: Habits and Willpower

"There's nothing you can't accomplish if you get the habits right." — **Charles Duhigg**

Our lives are the direct result of all the habits we have developed over time. Whether the habit is filling your bowl full of M&Ms while working at your desk or checking your emails while running on the treadmill, your habits have shaped you into who you are right now.

A key term often mentioned frequently when it comes to habit change is 'willpower.' What is your willpower, and what role does it play in the entire habit-building process?

The Magical Potion Named 'Willpower'

Many of us firmly believe our lives would become awesome if we had more willpower. With more self-control, we could all exercise for an hour daily, avoid smoking, be more productive, save more for retirement, and achieve all our noble goals.

A survey conducted by the American Psychological Association on stress asked the participants the number one reason for not being successful in achieving a healthy lifestyle. 27% responded that the lack of self-control was the biggest hurdle to that process.

Respondents also believed willpower is a learned behavior and that they could build better willpower if they had more time for themselves. However, they also thought that willpower does not automatically grow when you have more time in the day.

According to research, a lack of willpower is not the primary reason we cannot actualize our goals. Three more elements you need to bring about the anticipated changes in your life include:

(1) **establishing the motivation** for the habit change along with a clear, concise goal;

(2) **monitoring your behavior** and performance targeted towards that particular goal, and lastly;

(3) working on **shaping your willpower.**

According to the research results, willpower is quite an integral part of the equation, but it is not the only necessary element.

Willpower is your ability to resist something in the face of temptations. Every time you try to stick to your plan of implementing a habit change, you experience some resistance.

The resistance could be an ill feeling, the temptation to do something that feels easier or more enjoyable, or a period of demotivation.

You must manage those temptations and frictions to achieve your desired goal. That is what your willpower helps you do.

Psychologists Angela Duckworth (Grit) and Martin Seligman (Learned Optimism), both PhDs and working at the University of Pennsylvania, discovered that individuals with better self-control tend to lead better lives.

They conducted research that involved assessing the ability to exercise self-control in eighth-graders. They assigned a task to students, giving each student the option of receiving $1 immediately after completing the assignment or $2 the following week. Those who chose to wait for a week to receive an extra dollar reported having better grades, higher standardized test scores, and better attendance; they also got into better high school programs.

How Does Your Willpower Affect You?

Regulating your willpower is the purview of the pre-frontal cortex, which is a part of your brain that evolved later than many other brain regions. The pre-frontal cortex is the part where decisions about what temptation to avoid and what decision to make happen.

Your prefrontal cortex fires up whenever you need to decide something associated with a habit change. It allows you to focus on why that habit change matters, allowing you to exercise self-control.

Your pre-frontal cortex is valuable to you but consumes significant energy. Thus, every time you need to exercise self-control, your pre-frontal cortex starts to use your power. As the day moves on, you continue to consume energy. Since you are also using power in other tasks and functions such as focusing, decision-making, analytical thinking, problem-solving, and taking actual action, you start running low on energy after a while

Eventually, you get to a point where you start functioning on reserve willpower, and then it too depletes. This explains why it sometimes becomes tougher to tap into your willpower, especially when you need to push yourself harder to achieve a milestone. It may be easier to jog for 10 minutes since you have been doing that for a month. However, jogging for 15 minutes may require more willpower and energy, which is why it feels more complicated. Imagine doing it on a day when you feel sleep-deprived and have work stress to tackle.

Your willpower is a vital resource but a finite one. You cannot rely on it at all times to get to where you envisage. You need self-control to stick to the right path and keep doing what you wish to do and achieve. How can you manage that? Let's take a look.

Willpower and Self-Discipline

It becomes challenging to exercise willpower because your prefrontal cortex is energy-hungry. The ability to exercise your will refers to self-control. The more self-control you need to practice, the more energy your pre-frontal consumes, and the more drained you feel. This applies to each one of us. Even the most successful people who have complete control over their lives still struggle with it. However, they still get their work done because they know an elixir called 'self-discipline.'

You may be thinking that willpower and self-discipline are the same things. Most people use the two terms interchangeably, making it seem like they're the same, but they are not.

If you go by the dictionary meaning, willpower means "to have control of your impulses and actions" and is also called 'self-control.' Self-discipline refers to training and disciplining yourself for personal improvement.

Willpower is about showing self-restraint when you need to do the right thing to steer clear of whatever may be tempting you from a chosen path. Eating healthy and avoiding junk food is the right thing when you are on a weight loss regimen. Whenever you feel an urge to eat a juicy beef burger with two cheese slices, you need self-control to not give in to this temptation.

To exercise that self-restraint, you need to have self-discipline. Self-discipline is about doing things that help you stick to your goal and practice self-control whenever you need it.

The different measures you take to stay in control of your temptation help you build self-discipline. Continuing with our example of resisting the temptation of not eating a burger, you could discipline yourself by having some delicious, healthy meals ready for moments when you want to eat some junk. You could also leave sticky notes full of encouraging statements such as "I stick to my goal," "I eat healthy food," or "Healthy food is delicious," to surround yourself with firm reminders.

Hence, self-discipline lays out the measures you can take to sculpt self-control to ensure you can easily carry on with the good habit you are trying to develop. Thus, to build the self-control you need to bring about a habit change, you must work on disciplining yourself. This also explains why self-control and self-discipline go hand in hand.

How to Build Self-Discipline

The key to becoming a more disciplined version of yourself lies in creating robust systems that keep you strong and motivated and help you think straight even when your willpower is crying for mercy.

Here's a *process* for what you need to do:

Take out your journal, and **read about the habit change** you want to implement first.

Analyze the habit change profoundly and, once again, reflect on the associated whys.

Think of the possible temptations you can encounter during the journey. For example, you are trying to work 8 hours a day as a freelance graphic designer while working from home. What could distract you from putting in that work? Perhaps you have a cluttered workspace that affects your productivity. Maybe you have a habit of using social media during your work hours. You may also get interrupted by friends showing up at your place.

After **contemplating the contingencies and distractions** that could come up, write them down, one after the other. These are times when you are likely to have a conflict with your temptations to exercise self-control.

For each of these distractions, **think of ways to combat them**. For example, you could block social media sites during work hours to keep yourself from using them. You could also log out of your accounts such that the thought of signing in again deters you from using them right away, and perhaps even have an accountability buddy who reminds you of your target time and again.

Next, **brainstorm ways of giving yourself gentle reminders** to execute these activities every time your self-control is in jeopardy. You could set reminders on your phone, put up notes in your house, and ask your accountability partner to check in with you now and then.

Also, **examine your environment** for factors that may trigger your bad habit or tempt you into giving in to your urges. Maybe there is a TV in your room, and seeing it makes you binge-watch TV for hours. Perhaps you have put up some cool posters about social media in your room that unconsciously lure you towards your socials.

You would also need to **build a tighter grip on your emotions** and the tendency to please others to stay disciplined. Most of us struggle with saying no to others, even when we are right.

Perhaps a friend shows up unannounced and asks you to accompany him to run his errand. While you have work to do, you still agree to go with him only to please him. If you are a people pleaser or cannot decline to help others just because you are that 'nice guy', this scenario will resonate well with you. It is okay to feel that way, but remember, you can only accomplish your goals once you focus more on your needs and targets and less on other peoples' needs.

Every time someone approaches you for a favor at a time when you have personal things to do or take care of, **politely turn them down**. Learn to say NO more often than you say YES. Take a deep breath, think of your goals and higher obligations, and tell the other person how busy you are and cannot oblige to their request.

Do not deviate from your position, and do not give excuses either. Be clear, precise, and firm; soon enough, you'll get the hang of saying no to others when needed. Yes, help others out when you have the time for it, but never at the cost of your work and productivity.

Remove all distracting elements from your environment to ensure it remains stripped of anything that jostles you towards your temptations.

Now **go over your daily work and life routine** and create a schedule that supports your habit change. Add in the practices you need to engage in to build a good habit or change a bad one, along with their starting time and total duration.

In the same schedule, **write down bullet points** detailing what you must do when your temptations try to tempt you. Once you have created an entire system of building self-discipline to fuel your self-control, start working on it.

You can **plan and strategize** as much as you want, but you get results only when you walk the walk. Start implementing your self-discipline plan to build the best habits for happiness, success, wealth, and more to become truly empowered.

While working on building healthy and positive habits, many people come across different statements and views that shake their willpower. Although many such statements are mere myths, they can trigger self-doubt and demotivate you.

Next, the following chapter busts six of the biggest **habit-related myths** to make your habit change process smoother and more enjoyable.

Chapter 5: Six Habit Myths Busted

Bringing about a habit change tends to be a tricky process. It is that way because we keep allowing certain myths to fool us. Like everything else, there are certain myths centered on habits as well.

In this chapter, we will tackle six of the most notorious habit myths and debunk them to give you a chance to push your way forward toward building the most empowering habits for success, health, wealth, happiness, and abundance.

Habit Myth #1: Lack of Willpower Leads to Building Bad Habits

When most of us fail to eliminate our bad habits, we usually blame it on our weak willpower. About one-third of the people in the US believe they don't have the necessary self-control to achieve their objectives. Around one-fourth find it challenging to stick to their diet regimen due to "their" laziness.

While you may think your lack of self-control is why you hardly ever achieve your goals, the truth is far from that. Almost 50% of the tasks we execute daily are chores we do unconsciously. That means we act without thinking very much.

Studies also show that those with high self-control are not battling their temptations 24/7. They rely more on good habits that keep them on the right track.

Thus, self-control is a mere illusion of a bedrock of different habitual patterns.

Once the patterns become habitual over time, you find it easy to follow them, and that's how your self-control grows. So, struggling to wake up early for work daily or failing to save money is not something you should blame on "weak" self-control.

Habit Myth #2: Apps Can Help You Improve Your Behaviors

Apps have attained quite a permanent status in our lives. We have an app ready at our disposal for everything we want to achieve, be it meditating, eating healthy, practicing intermittent fasting, tracking daily expenses, or even journaling our thoughts.

Since they are so easy and convenient to use, many people believe apps can undoubtedly help us build and improve different behaviors. Book Lover, MyFitnessPal, Fitbit, and other similar apps are well-known for improving people.

At a base level, apps help you monitor what you are doing. Monitoring your behavior enables you to identify your shortcomings and track your performance, but it does nothing much in yielding permanent behavior change. Scientists believe there is a substantial gap between recording information and carrying out a noticeable behavior change.

If you are not doing something meaningful about a specific habit and only focusing on monitoring yourself, it won't produce any lasting and remarkable effect. Hence, it is wise not to rely on apps to change your unhealthy behaviors. You can use them to track your performance, but do not expect them to improve you in a fortnight without much effort.

Habit Myth #3: It Always Takes 21 Days to Build a Habit

The idea that you can build or break a habit in only 21 days stems from a book on habits by Maxwell Maltz. Many self-help books vow you can fix your money issues, get a leaner body, and ditch smoking in only three weeks.

Yes, it takes about 21 days to get accustomed to a specific behavior you are trying to build or change, but there is no fixed, magic number for building habits. Certain behaviors take fewer days to grow roots in your life, while others take longer.

A study showed that people who wanted to start drinking water before meals took 18 days to build the habit. On the other hand, another study shows that building a regular exercise habit took the respondents closer to one full year. On average, it takes about 66 days to form a new habit.

For many of us, establishing a routine with well-defined systems is the thing that works best in building or breaking habits. It is not about the number of days you work but the time and location you execute the activity.

A study comprising regular exercisers showed that 90% of them used the time or location of the exercise as a cue to trigger that habit; exercising was an automatic behavior that required less willpower and thought.

If you have worked on a practice trying to change into a habit for 21 full days, but are still struggling to do it automatically, give yourself some more time and be consistent; the new routine will break in eventually. Just keep working on it, and you will reach the finish line.

Also, the time it takes for different people to work on a habit varies. It may take 30 days for you to build a strong habit, but it may take your friend 90 days to build the same pattern. Just be patient with yourself and keep going forward.

Habit Myth #4: Setting Realistic Goals is the Only Way to Change Habits

Regarding habit change, experts opine that you must set realistic goals. A study on the subject shows that those who wish to change habits prefer getting a book on goal-setting instead of one on environmental change.

The truth is quite the opposite to this:

Setting realistic goals is crucial to replacing bad habits with good ones, but that does not change the truth that your environment also plays a substantial role in remaking your behavior. If you change the cues that trigger unwanted behavior, you can break the respective habits too.

If your favorite cafeterias replace unhealthy snacks with healthy ones, you will likely eat less harmful food. If you have a treadmill right next to your desk, you will probably walk/jog on it more than if you had no treadmill.

A study conducted on veterans of the Vietnam War revealed the importance of our environment. 20% of them had heroin addiction while they served overseas. Of these, 5% relapsed on returning home. Researchers believe this stark change was due to the drastic change in their environment.

Habit Myth #5: Knowing the Benefits of New Habits Changes Your Behavior

This is another common myth regarding habit change. People believe that if you know the benefits of any new habit you wish to cultivate, you will successfully build that particular habit.

To make the masses eat more greens and vegetables, the Federal Government launched the 'Fruits & Veggies, More Matters' in 2007. As impressive as the campaign seems, it did not work —at least not as effectively as they had hoped. Since 2007, the consumption of fruits and vegetables has decreased. Research has time and again shown the same. Educating people regarding the advantages of a specific behavior only increases their awareness; it does not translate into a habit change.

Habit formation happens through actually doing things. The long-term memory systems involved in developing habits do not change with new resolutions. Researchers have discovered that associations with old habits endure, obstructing behavioral changes even when adopting a new intention.

Habit Myth #6: You Can Only Quit Habits the Cold Turkey Way

A prevalent misconception associated with habits is that the cold turkey way of quitting an addiction is the only way to do it. For example, you can either quit smoking right away or not. The "slow and gradual" approach does not work. This is nothing but a myth.

In his bestselling book, 'Atomic Habits,' James Clear talks about how making small, incremental changes to old habits brings about a compound effect in the long run. Going all-in on a positive habit or quitting a negative habit cold turkey are extreme measures that rarely yield positive results.

These myths have long prevented many people from working on changing their unhealthy habits. Probably, they affected you in similar ways. Now that we have debunked them, you will find it easier to get rid of them.

Let us move on to the first **self-care habits** in the following chapter.

Part 2: Health Habits

"Good habits are the key to all success. Bad habits are the unlocked door to failure."

—Og Mandino

Chapter 6: The Sleeping Habit

"I love sleep. My life tends to fall apart when I'm awake, you know?" — **Ernest Hemingway**

I don't know about you, but this is certainly a sentiment many people share. Good sleep is something many of us yearn for, and it is also something we often don't get a lot of in this modern age of busy people. No, that's not because of some sleep deprivation virus spreading around. Poor sleep or lack of sleep does boil down to poor sleeping habits, which many of us are guilty of.

This part of the book focuses on the many self-care habits you can build to better care for yourself and become physically, mentally, and emotionally healthy.

The Need to Sleep Well

According to the American Association of Sleep, adults need anywhere between seven and nine hours of sleep to function optimally. If you sleep for fewer hours than that, it slowly deteriorates your physical and mental health.

Here's what sleeping well daily does for you:

- It boosts your immune system

- It keeps your gut healthy and prevents you from getting sick often

- It helps you maintain a healthy body weight

- It reduces stress

- It improves your emotional well-being and mood

- It improves your concentration

- It enables you to think clearly and practice good problem solving

- It helps you to feel fresh and active throughout the day

- It reduces the likelihood of developing health issues such as heart problems and diabetes

For all these reasons, and to be a better person for the people around you, sleeping well is essential. We cannot deny that we tend to become a ticking time bomb when we are in a bad mood due to poor health and dysfunctional mental cognition.

Now, here is how you can build the habit of sleeping well.

How to Build the Habit of Sleeping Well

If you have trouble sleeping soundly at night and constantly get up many times during the six to nine hours you need to be sleeping and dreaming; it is evident you haven't worked on building the sleeping habit.

Don't worry. With this book by your side, you can quickly build this habit. Here are the essential mini habits you need to start working on to get quality sleep daily.

Plan Your Day the Night Before

Many of us make the mistake of planning our next day when it starts. You start your day thinking of what to achieve, which consumes most of your energy and time even before starting your tasks for the day.

Since planning takes up time from the actual chores, you later have to make up for them by sacrificing your sleep. Things would become more manageable if you started planning your day the night before, ensuring you could crawl into your bed on time. This also lets you plan for bedtime so you drift asleep immediately.

To build this habit, here's what you must do:

- Every night before your bedtime, schedule in 15 minutes and sit somewhere quiet.

- Take your journal and think about what you must do the next day.

- Put down all your deliverables (priority tasks) along with a clear schedule for what time you intend to do them.

- Go through the activities several times to ensure you don't miss anything important.

- Set the alarm or notification through your Google calendar to work on this habit.

- Schedule all the energetic activities for at least 3 to 4 hours before your scheduled bedtime. Physical activities or any chore that creates an adrenaline rush leads to an overflow of excitement in the body that plays havoc with your sleep cycle. Schedule such activities for early to mid-day to ensure you feel tired closer to bedtime and can sleep easily.

Create a Sleeping Schedule with 6 to 8 Sleeping Hours

Adults need between 7 to 9 hours of sleep, but 6 to 8 hours daily will work fine. A strict sleeping schedule will ensure that you feel sane enough to work throughout the day. Here's how you can build this habit:

- If possible, sleep for 6 hours, 7 hours, 8 hours, and then 9 hours on four different days. Regarding your workload and activities, try to keep everything else on those days the same.

- Analyze your energy levels, mood, and performance at work on those days to figure out your optimal sleep requirement. Some people function well on sleeping 6 hours, while others work best when they get 8 hours. On the other hand, some people feel drowsy after sleeping for 9 hours straight but function optimally after a 7-hour sleep.

- Once you have discovered your optimal sleep requirement, set a sleep time and rising time that allows you to sleep for that duration.

- Go to bed 15 to 30 minutes earlier than your sleep time.

- Put away your phone and take deep breaths to concentrate better on relaxing.

- I recommend practicing <u>Yoga Nidra guided meditation</u> to help with falling asleep.

- Wake up at the set time, even if you haven't slept well during the night. It will take a couple of days for your circadian rhythm to adjust to this new routine, but soon you'll accomplish this goal.

Create a Sound Sleeping Environment

To build a habit of sleeping sufficiently and soundly, develop a habit of creating a comfortable sleeping environment first.

- Check the temperature of your room and adjust it according to your needs. Low temperature promotes good sleep, but you can keep it just how it suits you.

- Toss out all sorts of electronics and gadgets from your room. Avoid bringing such items into your bedroom to ensure your space becomes a sleep haven devoid of any distractions and you feel relaxed the instant you enter it. However, if you have a small apartment and no place else to work but from your bed, put your electronics away an hour before bedtime. Blue rays from screens disturb your circadian rhythm (responsible for many things, including sleep). Hence, it is important to limit your screen time, especially before bedtime.

- Dim the lights in your room at least 30 minutes before your sleep time.

- Play light music or soothing nature sounds in your room before bedtime to help you unwind. If this does not work for you, you do not need to practice it.

- Check if your bed, mattress, sleeping covers, sheets, pillows, and other bedding items are comfortable enough to initiate sleep.

Check these things regularly to help yourself find it easy to sleep.

Meditate Before Bedtime

Meditation is a calming practice that helps your mind and body become one, allowing you to live in the moment. It relaxes your mind, steers you away from tensions, and enables you to do whatever you wish to do in the present.

Meditating before bedtime is a great way to cleanse your mind of chaotic and stressful thoughts that divert your attention from sleep. Here's how you can practice it:

- Sit in your bedroom at least 30 to 40 minutes before your bedtime.

- Say, 'I am going to meditate peacefully' about ten times.

- Close your eyes while keeping your hands on your side.

- Inhale through your nose to a count of 5.

- Feel your breath as it circulates in your body, and pay full attention to it when you inhale.

- Exhale through your mouth to a count of 6 or more. Exhaling out more air relaxes you better.

- Watch the out-breath just as you observed your in-breath.

- Breathe like this for ten complete cycles or 5 to 10 minutes for better results. Since it can be difficult to meditate for 10 minutes right away, start by meditating for 30 seconds, then increase it to 60 seconds, and then a couple of minutes.

- Practice Yoga Nidra guided meditation or the Silva Method.

Stick to this practice and see how it makes you feel. You are likely to feel calmer and more mindful than ever; you may also find it easier to doze off comfortably. A good night's sleep is only some mini habits away. Follow the guidelines above, and you'll be happy you invested in this new way of life you're creating for yourself.

Let us move to the next set of self-care habits...

Chapter 7: The Eating Well Habit

"We are our own potters; for our habits make us, and we make our habits." — **Frederick Langbridge**

Do you think the word "health" is self-explanatory and we overthink what it means to be healthy? Do you have an explanation of human well-being, or do you also think that committing to diets like Keto or Carb-Cycling is the best approach?

New diet concepts have caused a whole lot of confusion for people. When asked about fitness, you come up with descriptions you read on social media and never view the question from a layman's perspective. Don't you think there should be some simple reasoning that anyone can make sense of?

Before you form your judgment, you must know why a healthy intake is essential. By the time you'll see the outcome of acquiring healthy eating habits, you will have your definition and answer.

Why Do I Need to Make Healthy Food Choices?

"Food is one of the most important tools for a life lived well — and long."

This means food directly impacts your life.

A proper diet gives you the strength to manage your mental health, fight diseases, and shape your body. Chronic diseases, depression, and obesity are common because of poor nutrition.

These outcomes are all interconnected because they emerge from a single cause. If you fix it, you will overcome these problems and lead a fulfilling life.

How to Improve Eating Practices

The problem isn't your cravings; your negligence fuels your cravings. You don't discipline yourself and end up over-filling yourself with non-nutritious food. The challenge is to prioritize what to eat and when to eat.

Consider the following initiatives to kickstart your journey towards better eating.

Plan Your Meals Ahead of Time

It saves you from confusion and time wastage when deciding what to eat. When you have a specific plan, you anticipate the experience of having it while working. Your mind automatically prepares you for the meal and gives you the determination to stick to it. In short, it keeps you from getting carried away with thoughts of unhealthy food.

Also, ensure you have the ingredients for your meal; otherwise, it becomes disappointing. Nobody likes changing plans at the last moment.

Plan a Weekly Nutritional Meal Chart

Sit and jot down your favorite healthy foods and make a good grocery list. Buy all your ingredients in a single shopping trip and schedule your meals. This way, you'll know what you will have for your breakfast, lunch, and dinner if you set yourself up to prepare it better.

Also, keep in mind the importance of every meal timing. Your breakfast starts your day, so it should provide plenty of energy. It's advisable to choose protein and fiber and not ruin breakfast with high-fat or calorie foods.

Have a moderate lunch, including the rest of the nutrients, and always take a light dinner. By light, either limit your portion size or take easy-to-digest foods. Steamed vegetables with grilled chicken would be a great option.

Pack (From Home) What You Need for Each Day

Taking lunch from home gives you more control over your available food choices. When you take some extra time out of your morning schedule to prepare yourself some lunch, you will not let it waste.

This planning connects with your weekly chart. The more time, energy, and resources you invest in your weekly chart, the easier it will be to gain control over your eating pattern.

Eat One Piece of Fruit or One Serving of Raw Vegetables Mid-Morning and Mid-Afternoon

Include fruits and vegetables in your diet. Try having them as close to their original form as possible. Don't make juices out of them or use them in pies.

Consume natural foods as they are to gain maximum nutritional benefit. It's not compulsory to add them to your main course. You can make a salad for your mid-day snack and decorate it with some salad dressing to make it appealing and attractive.

A vegetable and fruit-rich diet lowers the risk of heart diseases and vitamin deficiency, prevents various cancers, and controls blood sugar and digestive problems. Some recommended vegetables and fruits are cucumbers, celery, broccoli, apple, blueberries, kale, avocados, citrus fruits, leafy green vegetables, etc.

Pack a Healthy Snack for the Ride Home from Work

When you are heading back from work—tired and sleepy—you don't feel like going to the kitchen to make something. Instead, ordering in seems more convenient, and you usually get junk food. Such occurrences disrupt healthy habits, more so when there is no planning.

There are days when you don't want to cook, and it's completely fine. You can switch to alternatives like getting something healthy from outside, but don't let this laziness completely control your food choices. On lazy days, keep some healthy food options in mind to switch to, and avoid getting any processed food.

Don't even look at any drive-thru; instead, pretend fast food restaurants don't exist!

Shop from the Outer Rim of the Grocery Store

Have you ever wondered whether you are shopping at a grocery store the right way? You tend to spend most of the time inside the store walking between the aisles when you should be outside the store getting fresh food like meat and dairy.

The midsection of any grocery store is where you will find all the processed and canned foods. It is mainly the outside perimeter of a store where they keep the fresh supply. Try getting as many products from the outer counter as possible, and don't roam inside. This way, you will not deviate from your plan.

A healthy lifestyle has a huge payoff; fortunately, it's not hard to achieve. With persistence and determination, you will get addicted to it and wonder why you didn't do it before. After fixing your diet and feeling great about your new food choices, let's keep moving forward into…

The **Exercise and Fitness** habit.

Chapter 8: The Exercise/Fitness Habit

"The trick to success is to choose the right habit and bring just enough discipline to establish it."

— Gary Keller and Jay Papasan

A physically fit body allows you to carry out your routine chores effectively and live a healthy life. Sleep and a good diet certainly contribute to your physical and mental health. Exercise plays a vital role in the equation. As much as we understand the importance of exercising, not many of us do it regularly.

Self-care involves giving your body the necessary care, which happens best when you move around sufficiently and stay active. Sadly, many of us live sedentary lives characterized by low mobility, more reliance on technological gadgets, and now working from home courtesy of COVID-19. As relaxing as this lifestyle may sound, it is detrimental to your health and well-being.

Why Build the Habit of Exercising?

Exercise helps you stay fit and active. It improves your agility and mobility, thereby improving your quality of life. Here is how the habit of exercising regularly adds value to your life:

- It boosts cognitive health

- It improves heart health

- It reduces the risk of diabetes, high blood pressure, and heart problems

- It strengthens your immune system

- It clears mental and brain fog

- It alleviates stress, anxiety, and depression

- It improves your emotional and mental wellbeing

- It increases your stamina and physical strength

- It helps you manage your weight and better manage obesity-related conditions.

- It improves your efficiency and overall productivity

If you want to reap all these benefits of exercise, it is time to build an exercise habit.

How to Build the Exercise Habit

My goal is to simplify things for you. While exercising may seem like a tedious activity or something you need to put in much effort for, you can build the habit by focusing on a few mini habits.

Set a Fixed Time Daily

Just like you need to understand the cue of a habit to replace it, you need to set an alert for building a new habit.

Habits grow well when fed with punctuality. When you do a specific task at a fixed time every day, it will soon become habitual. Right at 5 PM, you would want to have your evening tea or meditate if those are the habits you have anchored to that time. The same applies to building the habit of exercising.

Use time as a cue to trigger this habit so that you feel the urge to exercise every time the clock strikes 6 PM or 8 AM.

Here's what you need to do:

Find a **convenient time you can dedicate to exercising**. Choose a time when you don't have anything pressing to do.

Make sure to **pick a time when you can dedicate** about 10 to 15 minutes, if not more, to exercising. It could be in the morning, noon, afternoon, or evening. Late evening and night are not ideal because exercising close to bedtime puts you in a hyper mode that disrupts your sleep cycle.

Stick to this time daily by setting up alarms and reminders and leaving sticky notes around the house.

Start with this bit of practice, and in about 3 to 4 weeks, you will develop the automatic urge to exercise at the set time.

Start Small

"The journey of a thousand miles begins with a single step."
— *Lao Tzu*

To complete a one-mile walk, you need to take the first step. Similarly, to exercise for 60 minutes straight, you must start with a minute or two. If you have been sedentary for a long while, it will be overpowering for you to push yourself to exercise for an hour right away.

Taking baby steps is the best way to go forward:

- Dedicate 5 to 10 minutes to exercising.

- Choose any rigorous physical activity. You could do aerobics, Zumba, Yoga, Pilates, kickboxing, swimming, play tennis, or anything else that makes your heart race and causes you to break a sweat.

- If you can hit the gym, do so. You can discuss your workout regimen with your fitness instructor or choose one according to your body type by spending some time researching on Google.

- Every day at the set exercise time, start working out. You could even walk or jog for 5 minutes if engaging in aerobics or running on the treadmill isn't your thing.

This may seem too small for now, but trust me, working out for 5 minutes every day is a considerable achievement. In weeks, you will notice fantastic results in your glowing skin, increased stamina, and better mood.

Keep Your Shoes Ready

Another mini habit that does a great deal at helping you develop the habit of exercising is to have your shoes ready. If you cannot easily find your shoes when you need to work out, you may panic, pace around the house in a frenzy, and, ultimately, feel demotivated to go out for your run.

On the contrary, if your shoes are ready by the door, you'll quickly slip into them and leave on time for your workout/exercise routine.

- Clean your workout shoes the night before.

- Keep them close to the door with a fresh pair of socks every night to ensure you don't shift to frantic searching mode close to your exercise time.

- If tying the shoelaces is annoying, choose 'sock shoes' or sneakers with velcro straps.

- Similarly, keep your workout clothes/tracksuit fixed to ensure you can easily find them when needed.

- On returning home from your workout or after exercising at home, please take off your shoes, clean them, and immediately place them at the chosen spot.

- Keep your at-home exercise equipment in your workout area, like an exercise mat, dumbbells, etc.

Start working on this habit, and then assess how much ease it adds to your life. This one little habit can make it easier to exercise daily.

Just Head Out the Door

Just as you build the habit of keeping your shoes and workout clothes ready, build another micro habit of heading straight out the door when it is time to work out. If your exercise time is 4 PM, move directly to the main entrance when the alarm beeps or after the clock strikes 4.

If you get the urge to do anything else or any other chore, ignore it and do what you had planned. This spontaneity to get straight to your workout is an enabler that helps you successfully build the habit.

Make It Pleasurable

When you add the element of excitement and fun to any activity, it becomes all the more enjoyable. This is true for exercise too. If you make it pleasurable, you become more involved and find it easier to stick to the habit.

It is important to discuss human psychology here. The human mind naturally gravitates toward intense emotions. Whatever you feel strongly, you remember better and become more engrossed in it. All the memories from the past with a solid emotional attachment are easier to recall. Similarly, you look forward to every activity you genuinely enjoy.

Keeping that in mind, it makes perfect sense to infuse some pleasure and excitement into your exercise regimen. Here are some ideas for you:

- Pick a different physical activity for every day of the week. Mondays can be cycling days, Tuesdays can be Pilates days, Wednesdays can be all about swimming, etc.

- Involve some friends in your workout routine. You could hit the gym with a buddy or two, ask them to accompany you on your run, or invite them to your place for a yoga session.

- Put on some music and groove to its beat, or work out to its tune.

- Work out in an outdoor venue such as a park, garden, or even a forest, if that is possible.

In addition, think of happy thoughts and memories when working out to make the experience all the more exciting.

Don't Miss Scheduled Days

Adopt a strict attitude towards your exercise schedule. Put the workout routine and the scheduled time on a planner and stick to it religiously. You can even peg a reward to it to incentivize yourself. Incentives have a magical effect on your subconscious, effectively pulling you towards your habit.

Have a Rest Day

Although it is essential not to miss a scheduled day, having a rest day between workouts is equally important. When you exercise and work out, your muscles experience wear and tear; they need rest to rejuvenate. If you keep working out for long hours without any rest day, you may push yourself towards a muscle, bone, or joint injury.

To stay fit and healthy while reaping all the benefits of exercise, institute a rest day during the week. For starters, 10 minutes workouts seven days a week is fine. You can even have two workout sessions of 10 minutes each six days a week. After two to three weeks, increase the duration to 15 minutes of workout/exercise sessions six days a week.

Gradually, stretch the duration to 40 minutes in about 4 to 8 weeks. Once you start working out for 40 minutes, ensure a day or two of rest during the week.

Track Your Progress

After a week of building the habits discussed above, start tracking your progress. The first few days must be about settling into the practice and getting to a point where you can do it without compulsion.

Once you have exercised for a couple of days, check your progress. Analyze if you have been performing a posture correctly, if you work out for the entire length of the workout time, or if you exercise with total energy or not.

Track your performance and progress weekly, then adjust your routine accordingly. Perhaps you do not find jumping jacks fun anymore, so you can replace them with planks or another exercise you like better and find more challenging. Maybe you can easily carry out three crunches sets, and now it is time to double the sets. Maybe working indoors is getting boring, and you need to step outside.

Check what works for you and what does not, and keep tweaking your routine, environment, and habit accordingly.

I understand that pushing yourself to exercise can be difficult at the start. You are not used to it, so it feels difficult, but if you keep pushing yourself to work out and give yourself a few days to settle in, you will see how wonderfully it changes your life. You will start feeling fresher, more active, happier, confident, and more proactive.

The next chapter discusses this vital habit paramount to taking better care of yourself...

The Water Habit.

Chapter 9: The Water Habit

About 60% of the human body is water. Water also forms the essential component of about 90% of our body's vital functions and processes. This makes staying hydrated vitally important. When your water levels drop, you become dehydrated, which brings about many problems.

This chapter talks about why and how to build the habit of improving your water intake.

Why Drink More Water?

Mild dehydration of as little as 2% affects your mood, reaction time, memory, energy levels, and concentration. Adding only a few glasses of clean drinking water improves your mood, emotions, cognition, and overall physical health.

Here are ten reasons why you must drink more water:

1. It Improves brain health, cognition, and memory

2. It Promotes smooth digestion that improves your gut health

3. It Increases the circulation of oxygen in your brain, especially to your brain, which improves your overall energy levels.

4. It Keeps your stomach full, leading to a feeling of satiation that consequently helps manage hunger

cravings, thereby allowing you to manage your body weight

5. Cartilage in the human joints is 80% water; hence, you lubricate your joints by staying hydrated.

6. Drinking more water regulates your overall body temperature

7. Increased water consumption dilutes the minerals in your urinary tract, which, in turn, decreases the risk of kidney stone formation

8. Sufficient water intake maintains a balance in vital minerals such as sodium, potassium, and others that your heart needs for optimal functioning

9. Improving your water intake strengthens your body's natural detoxification systems that eliminate harmful substances and wastes from your body through bowel movements, breathing, urination, and perspiration

10. Mild fluid losses alone can lead to brain contraction from the skull, resulting in migraines and severe headaches, so drinking more water prevents and manages headaches effectively

For all these reasons, it is important to start drinking more water. Ideally, you should consume around 8 to 10 glasses of water daily.

How to Increase Your Water Intake?

Working on the following mini habits will help you stay hydrated:

Create the Hydration Mindset

Start with building the hydration mindset. "What is that?" you may ask. Like a growth mindset makes you think about growing yourself and not limiting your potential, a hydration mindset focuses on keeping yourself well hydrated throughout the day.

The first step to achieving any goal is to build the right mindset. In this case, you need to set the intention to start drinking more water. Setting an intention alerts your subconscious and makes it embrace that suggestion.

Once your subconscious accepts something, it incorporates it into your belief system. As soon as something becomes a part of your belief system, it influences your thoughts, actions, and behavior.

Hence, building the hydration mindset reminds you of your intention to drink more water. Here's how you can make this mindset and develop the habit of practicing the intention.

- Take out your journal and think of how much water you'd like to drink ideally.

- Based on that amount of water, create an intention to improve your water consumption.

- Your intention should be present-oriented, suggesting you are making efforts in the present moment to drink more water. Instead of saying/writing, 'I will drink more water, write, 'I drink more water.'

- To this intention, add more specificity, meaning you need to describe the water you will consume daily. You can specify it in glasses, liters, or gallons —whatever works. For example, if you plan on drinking ten glasses of water, write, 'I drink ten glasses of water daily.'

Present-oriented and specific suggestions make your mind accept that whatever you say is the reality. Since the subconscious mind cannot discern between reality and imagination, it takes whatever you feed to it. Speaking and writing that you drink a certain quantity of water daily makes the subconscious mind believe that.

- Write down and chant the suggestion ten times to embed it in your subconscious.

- Read this intention about ten times every day and end the day on the same note.

Soon, you'll chant this suggestion on autopilot and start acting accordingly.

Carry a Water Bottle at All Times

You check your phone constantly because you always have it on you. Likewise, if you carry a water bottle, you will probably drink more water. Get into the habit of filling a water bottle in the morning and always have it in your bag. You can keep it in your purse, laptop bag, or briefcase.

To ensure you remember to keep the bottle, use reminders, alarms, and sticky notes. Also, you can fill the water bottle at night and keep it on your dining table or alongside your office bag to ensure you remember to carry it wherever you go.

Keep Water in Your Office

Besides carrying a water bottle throughout the day, keep water in your office, study room, bedroom, and car. You may forget to take your water bottle occasionally, and in those times, the spare bottle at your office, in your car, and in other places will ensure you stay hydrated. This strategy also helps you drink sufficient water when your bottle runs out of water.

Drink 2 Glasses of Water Every Hour

Every two to three hours, drink about two glasses of water. If you go without water for long hours, gulping down two glasses in a single go may seem like a tough ask. In that case, drink half a glass every hour and slowly increase it to one full glass. Once you find it easy to drink a tall glass of water every hour, gradually make your way to drinking two glasses per hour.

If water seems too bland for your taste, you can drink flavored water or add fresh juices and smoothies to your diet.

Drink Water Before and After Meals

Another mini habit you need to work on is to drink water before and after meals. Drinking at least one full glass of water half an hour before your meal promotes digestion and keeps you hydrated. Also, have a few sips of water about 20 to 30 minutes after your meal.

Drinking water after a meal helps your body absorb the nutrients in the meal you consume. However, don't go overboard on consuming water after a meal as it can dilute your digestive juices, thereby hampering the smooth digestion process.

Begin and End Your Day with Water

After waking up, drink a glass of water before entering the bathroom. End your day with a couple of sips of water too. Avoid drinking full glasses of water at night because too much fluid leads to frequent urination, disrupting your sleep.

Work on any of these habits first, slowly adding more practice to your routine.

To build good habits for life, here's a recommended performance strategy.

Performance Strategy for Habit Stacking

It is good to tie together the different habits you have learned so far. Stacking one habit on top of another creates a series of patterns, each acting as a cue for the next one in line. For example, if you meditate before bed and sip your water after meditation, ending the meditation session acts as a reminder to drink water, which, in turn, cues you to get to bed.

Here is a set of performance strategies for the self-care habits discussed in this part of the book.

1. Start your day with a glass of water

2. Eat a nutritious breakfast

3. Pack in a healthy snack or two for work along with a bottle of water

4. Keep sipping water throughout the day

5. Walk whenever possible

6. Go for a jog/walk/workout at the scheduled time

7. Sip water or have a fresh juice/beverage

8. Have a healthy dinner

9. Drink some more water

10. Walk for a bit

11. Go to bed 15 minutes early

12. Check the environment of your bedroom, and ensure it is sound

13. Meditate for 5 minutes

14. Take a sip of water

15. Go to bed

You have the liberty to tweak this strategy and sequence based on your personality, needs, and interests.

In addition, when you work on the different habits discussed in this book, make and note down the following observations:

Duration: See for how long you practice that respective habit. If you are meditating, and the idea is to meditate for 15 minutes, time yourself each time you meditate. If you meditate for 1 minute in the first week, note that down. If you slowly progress to meditating for one and a half minutes, write that down. Doing this helps you track your performance, ensuring that you gradually stretch it to the desired duration.

Best Time: Try a certain practice at different times of the day to see when you get the best results. Carrying on with the example of meditation, you can try it in the morning, noon, afternoon, evening, and night.

In each part of the day, practice it at different times too. Perhaps, you figure out that you are too tired at night to focus on meditation and do it better in the afternoon. This observation helps you find the most suitable time for all your habits, which allows you to get the best results.

Important Insights: Pay attention to how you execute a certain practice. Observe how you engage in a certain practice and how it affects your mood, behavior, and daily performance in other tasks.

Perhaps you find meditating outdoors distracting, and you meditate better in your room. Drinking two glasses of water may make you too full to enjoy your meal properly.

How to Perform: After analyzing yourself while carrying out different practices you wish to turn into lifelong habits, you will better understand the best way to perform them. That's when you can decide on the most appropriate approach to carry them out.

With a healthy body, you can take better care of your mind. You also need to build certain habits for **wellness and better thinking**, which is exactly what the next part of the book focuses on.

Part 3: Wellness and Thinking Habits

"Get on a daily routine... Working is a process not a product. Success comes from the word, succeed: Latin: 'to under go.' You must keep moving."

– Nicoletta Baumeister

Chapter 10: Wellness and Thinking for Better Life

"Your net worth to the world is usually determined by what remains after your bad habits are subtracted from your good ones." — **Benjamin Franklin**

Good habits often promote wellness in life. Everything we do and say, our minor actions and thoughts, all connect to the habits we have developed over time. Our repetitive behaviors have led to actions becoming our habits and, later on, our lifestyles.

Working on your wellness and thought process is the key to living a healthy and thriving life. Here is an analogy that will help you understand the importance of this:

To grow beautiful plants and flowers, you need to provide them with the right amount of sunlight, sufficient water, and fertile soil and nurture them well. You won't get gorgeous flowers if you don't do that right. Likewise, to be physically fit, mentally strong, and genuinely happy from within, you have to focus on your wellness and thinking habits.

If you struggle with thinking straight, have a cluttered state of mind, and strive to improve your emotional well-being, this part of the book will prove immensely helpful.

How Wellness and Thinking Habits Affect Us

A considerable part of negativity in our life comes from our toxic habits. We want to focus on our wellness, but the habits we have built over time do not yield those results.

Wellness focuses on our well-being and building healthy habits that help us become physically and mentally fit. That's how you can thrive in your life.

Deep thinking also has a vital role to play in this equation. When you think sincerely and rationally, you become more aware of yourself and your life. With that information, you understand what you need to improve on and start working on building habits conducive to wellness.

Let us discuss the habits you need to work on to promote wellness and deep thinking.

The Early Riser

One of the most productive habits of keeping yourself well is waking up early in the morning. "An early bird always gets the worm" is an old saying that reminds us of the benefits of waking up early.

Below are the steps you can take to build the habit of being an early riser:

Allow yourself to sleep earlier

"Early to bed, Early to rise. Keeps a person healthy, wealthy, and wise."

Most of us have heard this proverb throughout our lives, from nursery school, college, and beyond. Sleeping early will give your body and mind enough time to recover for the next day.

One cannot work efficiently and productively if they are tired. Sleeping at 10 pm and rising at 6 am gives you at least 8 hours of good sleep for the upcoming day. You'll be active, fresh, and energized before your daily work (and chores) begins.

Put your alarm clock far from your bed

Keeping the clock on your bed/bedside table makes it reasonably easy to turn the alarm off or snooze once it starts ringing, even doing so unconsciously. This leads to waking up late, being late for work/school, and is a bad start to your typical day.

On the other hand, keeping the clock far from the bed will wake you up properly because you need to get out of bed to switch the alarm off. Getting out of bed, stretching, and focusing on the objective (to turn the alarm off) will refresh your mind and work on the task.

Go out of the bedroom as soon as you shut off the alarm

The instant you've turned the alarm off, head towards the exit. Going back to sit or lay on the bed makes it very tempting to get back into bed for a little snooze. As soon as you've left the room, head towards the bathroom to freshen up. Drink a glass of room temperature water to quick start your metabolism.

Make waking up early a reward

When you're up at 6 am, you've got over 3 hours to spare before your work/college time. Use that time to your advantage. Have a glass of orange juice, and treat yourself to your favorite breakfast. Reward yourself for waking up early and motivate yourself to do the same tomorrow.

Take advantage of all that extra time

Being up early in the morning gives you ample time to do all the extra work you have been unable to do because of your busy schedule. Catch up with social media, watch the episode you missed yesterday, and analyze the trending fashions globally. Take a cool shower and clear your thoughts. Plan your day and work out each step beforehand.

The connect with nature habit

Now that you've freshened up and had a cool glass of water, you have ample time before you get busy with your daily routine. Let's go out for a walk, shall we?

Take a walk into the woods: Go for a pleasant walk/jog. Start your day productively by working all your muscles and getting the blood flowing. Stretch your body and release the built-up tension by exploring the beauty of nature.

Breathe open air: The purest air one can find is in the early morning, in parks, and around the woods. Clean air always freshens the body and the mind. Deep breathing exercises get your brain working more efficiently.

Listen to birds sing: In the early morning, one can always enjoy a good stroll outside with some natural music from the birds singing their songs. It's always beautiful to realize how they start in a perfect rhythm; by the time they finish, we're always hoping for more.

Chapter 11: The Meditation Habit

Many of us are in the habit of thinking of multiple things simultaneously; a phenomenon called the monkey state of mind that describes our habit of jumping from one branch of thought to another, similar to how a monkey constantly leaps from one tree branch to another.

When you have multiple thoughts on a loop, you find it hard to focus on just one thing. Many times, these thoughts pertain to your past or the future. You are either stressed about something that happened some days ago or many years before, or you are worried about some concern regarding the future. Either way, you are not living in the present moment.

The only thing certain in your life is the present moment. Nothing else is for sure. Sadly, so many fail to embrace the gift that is present, which is why we feel so frustrated, distraught, and unable to think clearly. Our wellness and the ability to think positively largely depends on our ability to live in the present.

You can nurture this ability in many ways, but practicing meditation is one of the best ways. Earlier on, we described meditation briefly. Let us dive into it in more detail in this chapter.

The Power of Meditation

Meditation brings forth a whole lot of goodness. Firstly, and most importantly, it instills a sense of mindfulness.

"What's mindfulness," you may ask?

I mentioned earlier how we often wander off in thought and may be doing things without focusing on the present moment. You may have noticed how you may be reading an email or making coffee but worrying about something else. Perhaps, there is an important upcoming meeting that feels intimidating, or you may be stressing about how to pay the bills this month, or there may be a gazillion other worries.

While behaving that way, we also tend to be overly critical and judgmental of the experiences we have in the present moment. You may want to try recording a song, but you continue being skeptical about it since you doubt yourself or are scared of how your family will receive it. You may want to talk to a new coworker, but you may judge her too since you have heard some nasty rumors about her.

We keep basing our opinion on different life experiences and moments based on our preconceived notions and fears. Even when we want to experience our lives fully, we do not do so because we are not living in the present mindfully.

Mindfulness is about embracing the present with everything it has and keeping a sense of acceptance as it unfolds. If you spill juice all over the kitchen counter, you do not see it as a sign of stupidity. Instead, clean it up and learn to be more careful next time.

If you wish to try your hand at starting your YouTube channel, you go ahead and embrace the idea because it feels exciting. You live in the moment and learn from it without being judgmental.

Moreover, mindfulness gives you the wings to fly above and beyond past and future concerns. What has happened is a bygone; what is yet to come is uncertain. You live in the present and should focus on that with clarity and devotion.

Once you start doing that, you feel peaceful, happier, more confident, more focused, and also become more productive. Instead of crying over spilled milk, you adopt a learning attitude. You strive for growth because you know mistakes happen and can do better by moving on.

Mindfulness gradually allows you to untie the knots of confusion in your head, slowly unravel the deep layers of doubts and fears, and move past your insecurities.

As you start to live more in the here and now, the present, you begin thinking clearly and rationally too. Clarity of thought allows you to explore and understand yourself better. With increased self-awareness, you start accepting and liking yourself better and get the courage to move towards self-improvement and growth.

That's how you start focusing better on developing the proper habits conducive to success and prosperity. Hence, mindfulness is one of the keys to living a good life.

Let's dive into how to build your meditation habit.

How to Build the Meditation Habit

With the help of some mini habits, you will be on your way to meditating like a pro. Trust me; it is way than you think. Just build the intention to meditate just like you built the hydration mindset. This time develop the meditation mindset by creating a powerful suggestion on how to meditate daily and enjoy it. Chant it regularly, and you'll feel an inner urge to meditate bubbling inside you quite soon.

After setting the intention to be more mindful and to meditate happily, here are the micro habits you need to direct your energies towards to develop this habit.

Put Your Phone on Airplane Mode

Before going to bed at night, set your phone on airplane mode. You won't receive messages and notifications once you put your phone in airplane mode. Without interruptions, you will quickly focus on thinking clearly and comfortably engage in your meditation practice.

Start as Soon as You Wake Up

It is easy to say that you will meditate every day, but saying it is not enough. We often forget to do the things we say we will do. Instead of just saying, do something about what you wish to do. Get into the meditation groove by setting a reminder to meditate immediately after waking.

After you have had a glass of water and freshened up a little after waking up, sit down to meditate. Stick a note reading, 'Let's meditate' on your bathroom mirror, nightstand, or anywhere prominent, and take a few deep breaths.

Meditate while sitting, standing, or even lying down. When it comes to meditation, there is no hard and fast rule on doing it. The posture and place do not matter all that much; how consistent you are and how focused you remain during the practice is what does.

Begin With 2 Minutes Only

Meditation requires self-control and focus. The feeling overwhelms you when you think of doing something for a long time. Since we are so used to multitasking, and thinking of scores of things at once, naturally, it doesn't feel easy to be attentive for 15 to 20 minutes consecutively.

Many beginner meditators make the mistake of meditating for a long duration at the start. When they constantly battle with maintaining their focus, they feel flustered, agitated, and confused. They then wonder, "meditation should be peaceful. Why, then, does it feel annoying?" That's a common concern for many novices.

The inability to focus well is not meditation's fault. The problem comes from a wrong approach to meditating. Adopt the '2-minute' approach to tackling all the complex tasks, even the new ones.

According to the approach, you need to just work on an activity for 2 minutes. 2 minutes isn't much, and you readily agree to practice the exercise, and once done with it, it does not scare you anymore. Soon, you start doing it often, and that's how you build a habit.

Similarly, sit down to meditate for 1 to 2 minutes. Stick to it for about a week or two. If it goes well, you can gradually move to more extended periods. That's when you can shift to meditate for 5 to 15 minutes in the morning. Always start small, and keep building your pace from there.

Stretch Before Meditating

Before beginning your morning meditation, it's important to get yourself into a relaxed, flexible state through stretching:

- Stand straight, feet at hip distance apart, and maintain this pose for a few seconds.

- Move your arms over your head, slowly bring them down and go as low as possible.

- Raise your right arm, and pull it towards your back with your left arm. Practice the same with the left arm.

- Bend both your legs a little, one after the other.

- After some light stretching for about 5 minutes, you can move on to your meditation practice.

Meditate Indoors or Outdoors

If you don't feel like getting out of bed, stay under the covers and meditate while lying in bed. You only have to focus on your breath, any room object, or just the sunlight peeking through the covers.

If you want to meditate outdoors, sit on the patio or your garden and meditate while observing any natural object, your breath, or just the feeling of early morning peacefulness.

Note Down Your Feelings

After meditating, even if it is for a minute, tune into your feelings and consider how you feel about a calming meditation session. Even if you kept drifting off in thought throughout the session, acknowledge those feelings. Practice and consistency will gradually help you start feeling more composed and calmer when meditating.

Note your feelings in a journal, notepad on your phone, or even talk about them and record yourself. Keeping a record of your emotions after meditation is an excellent strategy to track your performance and see how you continuously improve at the practice.

As you meditate better, your mind will become more apparent, making that an excellent time to build a deep-thinking habit.

Chapter 12: The Deep-Thinking Habit

"A person's mind is so powerful. We can invent, create, experience, and destroy things with thoughts alone."
— **Anonymous**

I have always found this quote very powerful. It reflects the power of thoughts. Your thoughts can help you make and break things, even your life. When something holds the force to make things, why break them, right?

To construct a beautiful life full of joy, you must clear your thoughts and build the habit of thinking profoundly and positively.

This chapter will help you do just that.

Why Build the Deep-Thinking Habit?

Deep thinking allows you to delve deeper into your emotions and make more sense of things. You may not understand yourself, your life, and the many problems you are stuck in only because you see what lies on the surface.

Perhaps you struggle with practicing good time management, but every time you attempt a new time management strategy, you fall short of committing to it. You fail to understand the reason behind the issue because you don't probe into the matter.

Maybe you don't have a clear sense of direction in life, which you find very bothersome. If you think about your genuine wants, desires, interests, and aspirations in life, you can connect the missing dots and find your purpose.

Deep thinking allows you to ponder on things, clarify different aspects of life, and analyze the various angles associated with a particular situation. Once you have a better perspective of things, you can comprehend them better and make logical, informed decisions.

Now that you know why you must think deeply let us talk about the mini habits that can assist you in developing this habit over time.

How to Build the Habit of Thinking Deeply

The ability to think profoundly is not a one-off thing. It is a habit you need to build with time by working on the following smaller habits that lead to it.

Start with Spending 5 Minutes with Yourself

Set aside 5 minutes daily for deep thinking without any judgment. This practice gives you time to clear your head, let go of cluttered thoughts, and contemplate pressing issues and just yourself.

Here's what you need to do.

- Pick 5 minutes at any time of the day when you are free. If you cannot find any time when you are free for even 5 minutes, just carve out 5 minutes from your lunch break or 5 minutes from the 15 minutes you go to bed early.

- Set alarms and reminders to engage in deep thinking at that time.

- When your thinking time approaches, grab your journal and sit in a quiet spot. Look for any corner in your house where nobody will disturb you for 5 minutes. If you cannot find any quiet spot, sit in your bathroom if you have to. You can even go to a park, sit in a library, or a quiet cubicle in your office.

- Once seated, take deep breaths for a few moments.

- After you have re-centered yourself, think about yourself.

- Start with the basics of who you are and how you define yourself.

- Think only of yourself and nothing else. Who are you? What do you want? Why are you in this life?

- Take each question at a time, and jot down whatever answers come to you, even if they do not make sense.

- If you feel like focusing on just one aspect or question in those 5 minutes, do so without probing further into other questions. Deep thinking is about taking your time with things, not rushing your thoughts.

Commit to engaging in this practice daily. Doing so will help you learn something interesting about yourself, your likes, passions, interests, and what moves you daily. Perhaps, you were already aware of those things but somehow had lost track of them. Deep thinking allows you to revisit who you are and indeed find yourself.

Once you start pondering on yourself, take this deep thinking up a notch, and think about the following:

- What is the purpose of my life?

- What am I meant to do?

- What sparks joy for me?

- What adds value to my life?

- In what direction am I headed?

- Am I genuinely happy and satisfied with my life?

- Am I developing the proper habits?

In addition, dig into whatever questions pop up in your mind and analyze them nonjudgmentally.

Question Basic Assumptions

Your next task is to question the basic assumptions you have. Whatever belief you have about anything in life, be it your purpose, interests, experiences you had on the road, or something you are confused about, consider all of them.

Every time you think of something you would like to explore, think of the following things:

- What does it mean to me?

- What does it mean in general?

- How do I feel about it?

- Where do my emotions for it stem from?

- What are the different aspects of it?

- Are the things I'm assuming right, or is there more to the equation?

Once you start questioning your basic assumptions, you will uncover the layers associated with an aspect. Your next task is to reason through logic.

Reason Through Logic

Reasoning through logic means that you do not jump to a hasty decision when you feel a certain way about an experience. Instead, you assess the situation and experience based on logical reasoning and try to make better sense of it.

Let's take the example of habit formation.

If you want to quit smoking but fall short of doing so every time you attempt it, do not just conclude that you can't stop. Instead, reason the situation with logic.

Think of what you are not doing right, what triggers the habit, whether or not you are managing the triggers well, how you can best overcome those triggers, why you give in to the urge, and similar factors associated with that habit.

The idea is to put your reasoning hat on whenever you face any situation. With time, the practice teaches you to find your way out of sticky situations, fix your problems, make better decisions, and do things you genuinely want, not those based on transitory whims.

Diversify Thought

Consider new angles and perspectives when pondering a problem or an experience.

- What do the different schools of thought think about it?

- How many different schools of thought exist on this topic?

- What is the cultural view of the situation?

- Is there any science behind it?

- What role do my emotions play?

- How will the situation change if some factors are removed or added?

Diversifying thought helps you examine a situation from multiple angles. Plus, it gives you more information to think critically and build your decision.

In addition, it exposes you to new information and engages perspectives on a situation. You comprehend a situation analytically and become better aware of your thought process. Also, you may end up getting new and exciting insights into yourself.

Be Aware of Your Mental Processes

Mental processes are the different things the human mind can do; being aware of them allows you to think analytically and critically. The standard cognitive processes usually encompass memory, perception, reasoning, thinking, emotion, and imagination.

It is crucial to be well aware of your mental processes because it helps you understand the following about your thought process:

- How you think

- The emotions you feel and how they influence your thinking and decisions

- How you perceive different things

- How you reason with yourself in a messy situation

- How strong or weak your imaginative capabilities are

- Whether or not you can logically analyze a situation under pressure

- How strong or weak your memory is, and the kind of memories that stir up in different situations

The Human mind is always active, even when we are asleep. That means our mental processes always affect our behavior, attitude, and decisions, making understanding them very important.

When you spend quality time thinking about yourself, dedicate time to closely looking at your mental processes.

Try Reversing Things

When things go south, we often shift to our panic mode. Things seem all haywire, and our mind starts to think frantically. After finding yourself in such situations, believing in the opposite direction is an excellent way to reverse things.

Evaluate the Existing Evidence

Many of us have the habit of reaching conclusions without considering the existing evidence on the matter.

You may think you are worthless without considering all your achievements in your past.

You may decide never to venture into a business again due to a couple of losses, forgetting that the loss happened due to your negligence and that you had previously achieved fruitful results when you acted diligently.

You may not pursue your lifelong passion for music only because some people think you are pathetic at it while forgetting all the beautiful melodies you have created that many people have loved.

Our judgments become skewed when we feel upset, experience a setback, or have undesirable results. We navigate towards the negative side of things and ignore all the positives that have come our way. Soon, we fixate on only the bad things in life; before we realize it, we feel overwhelmed with stress.

An excellent way to overcome this madness is to evaluate the evidence the minute things go wrong. Analyzing the proof associated with a situation, especially a setback, helps you account for everything that has happened. Instead of basing your judgment on mere assumptions, you use evidence to assess a situation and find a way to put your best foot forward.

Here's what you need to do to cultivate this habit:

- Take a few deep breaths to re-center yourself every time things take an undesirable twist.

- When you feel calmer, tell yourself, "It will be fine. I've got this." This calming suggestion helps you think positively and prepares you to hunt for evidence to support an argument or analyze a situation pragmatically.

- Next, ask yourself, "Do I have any evidence to support this argument?" For instance, if you want to shut down your business, consider why you should do that. Write down all the answers you get.

- After getting answers, do not settle on a decision before analyzing the other side of things. When shutting down your business, think of any achievements you have to your credit. You can ask yourself, 'Have I accomplished some profitable milestones?' Jot down the honest answers you get.

- Once you get some answers, think of how you successfully achieved those targets. What did you do right then? Once again, note down all your findings.

- In the same manner, analyze every situation, feeling, and emotion. If you feel incompetent, ask yourself why you feel that way, and then counter it by thinking of your good qualities. Think of the compliments people have given you over the years, and use them to have a debate with that inner critic inside you.

- After evaluating multiple sides of an issue with evidence, you can weigh all the different sides to conclude.

- Remember to be as unbiased as possible in this situation so you can make an objective and viable decision.

- If possible, get help from a trusted friend who can help you think logically with concrete proof.

Self-evaluation should be an ongoing practice whenever you face any situation that demands you to think logically and objectively. Try it a few times, set reminders to do so, and soon you will shift it to autopilot mode.

Remember to Think for Yourself

While you are busy evaluating and assessing things, you may tend to get distracted from your self. You may get too caught up in thinking of the best way to behave in a situation or what things mean to you that you stop thinking about yourself. When experiencing such situations, it is best to take a rain check on everything else to only focus on your needs.

Remember, you are the conduit of energy in your life. Your life revolves around you, and you are the one who shapes it a certain way. If it weren't for you, your life would be meaningless. You must always prioritize yourself to keep it moving in the right direction.

Now that we have discussed different habits for wellness and deep thinking let us move to the performing strategy that combines all the practices and gives you guidelines on how to take them as a whole.

Performing Strategy (Habit Stacking)

Habits work best when grouped and stacked. Here's a guideline to stack the wellness and deep-thinking habits:

- Wake up early and take a moment to acknowledge that feeling of rising early.

- Walk around the room for a bit to adjust to the reality of waking up.

- If you can go out into the woods, garden, or even on the patio, do so.

- However, if you cannot head outdoors immediately, sit down or lie on your bed and meditate for a full minute. Watch your breath during that time.

- Once you have meditated, head out for 5 minutes. Take a quick stroll around the block. If there are trees around, observe anyone for a couple of minutes.

- Come back indoors and sit peacefully.

- Dedicate 5 minutes to deep thinking about anything; you could also reflect on your little experience with nature outside just a few minutes ago. Think of what it means to you and how it impacted you, even though it was a brief interaction.

- You could also think of how to behave during the day or any pressing concern you have about yourself or your life.

- It is best to write it down to solidify those thoughts and not leave them hanging.

- Once done, take three deep breaths, observe them calmly, then get up and start the activities lined up for the day, starting with having a healthy breakfast.

Using these simple steps, you can have a powerful morning routine that energizes and prepares you for a productive day.

Remember one important thing: note down the best time, critical insights, the best way to perform a practice, and the duration of the respective practice while engaging in it. These insights help you better build the habit and keep it sustainable in your life.

After preparing your mind to think deeply and focus on your wellness, you need to start working on creating a positive mindset conducive to success and prosperity in life. Contrary to what the masses think, accomplishing this goal is relatively easy. With a few healthy habits broken into micro habits, you can build a brilliant mindset that will only lead to a thriving life.

Part 4: Mindset Habits

"Habit allows us to go from 'before' to 'after,' to make life easier and better. Habit is notorious – and rightly so – for its ability to direct even against our will; but by mindfully shaping our habits, we can harness the power of mindlessness as a sweeping force for serenity, energy, and growth."

– Gretchen Rubin

Mindset Habits: Introduction

"Once your mindset changes, everything on the outside will change along with." — **Steve Maraboli**

Your mindset encompasses your beliefs, opinions, and views shaping your thoughts, behavior, attitude, and actions. The cultivation of these elements shapes your life as a result. The mindset you nurture directly impacts all the other habits you build.

Why Setting the Right Mindset is Important to Practicing Other Habits

According to Stanford Professor Carol Dweck, there are two main kinds of mindsets: **growth** and **fixed**.

A fixed mindset makes you believe that your abilities and potential(s) are fixed traits, meaning you think you cannot change or improve them. You are likely to believe that being highly intelligent or talented is the only way to succeed in life —that hard work does not have any role in that regard. The growth mindset lies on the flip side of the equation.

With a growth mindset, you believe you can build your abilities, develop your talents and hone your potential(s) with time through hard work, effort, and consistency. Those with a growth mindset do not think they can become the next Steve Jobs. They believe that anyone and everyone can become more talented and innovative if they work at what they want.

You must nurture a growth mindset to do well in life, especially when building healthy habits. It gives you the courage to believe in yourself, the strength to keep going even when you slip up, and the positivity to discipline yourself in the face of temptation.

Building new habits and replacing old ones can be quite an uphill task for the better. There are days when we cannot walk an extra mile, drink more water, or hit the bed right at bedtime. On all such days, you may find yourself gravitating towards your temptations. Your judgment becomes clouded, and you may surrender to your unhealthy habits.

In such tricky times, your mindset comes to the rescue. You realize how you need to put in constant effort to achieve a goal. You know that some days may not be straightforward, and you must go the extra mile. You accept that it takes time to reach the finish line, but your hard work will never waste away. Thus, you keep trying, and that's how you gradually move to where you wish to be.

That is why you need to work on shaping the right mindset to build the proper habits. Let us now discuss the different mindset habits for a successful life in this part of the book.

Chapter 13: The Anti-Procrastination Habit

*"TRANSFORMATION is much more than using skills, resources, and technology. It's all about HABITS of mind." – **Malcolm Gladwell***

We have all had some bad days when our productivity went down the drain. No matter how hard you try, you do not have the strength to tend to your chores. It is okay. We have all been down that rabbit hole.

An occasional cycle of procrastination is normal. We need that break from working hard constantly. Not doing too much work once in a while is okay. However, if that becomes your go-to mechanism 24/7, and you start procrastinating on all your essential chores, that occasional procrastination turns into a habit, calling on you to change your gear, and go full speed on turning the tables on that bad habit.

Procrastination as a habit is more like termites in wood. It eats up your productivity, drains your strength, and depletes your motivation to move forward. To build good habits that empower you and help you make your best life, you need to work on building the anti-procrastination habit.

Let us look at some powerful, anti-procrastination habits that shape the 'can-do' mindset, so you can achieve anything you want.

Resolve Any Potential Emergency

Emergencies can be pretty messy. They disrupt your schedule and take you off track. You cannot anticipate all the possible contingencies that may come your way, but you can expect some and manage them.

Foreseeing some probably emergencies beforehand allows you to have a strategy or two in hand to tackle them in a timely manner. With the emergencies under control, you can efficiently work on your plan.

Here's how you can do that:

- Assess your schedule and milestones.

- Think about any unforeseen and unfortunate emergency that may pop up unannounced. For example, if you have a workout regimen to lose weight, think of what may happen when you sustain an injury. How are you going to lose weight if you have a sprained ankle?

- After thinking about some emergencies or foreseeing some coming your way, create an action plan to tackle them.

- Take care of the emergencies beforehand to reduce your risk and stress.

Work on this practice every few weeks or even weekly to have the upper hand on all the threats that may scare and stress you.

Do a Quick Daily Review

Every day, dedicate 5 to 10 minutes to reviewing your entire plan. Always go through all the daily targets, the deliverables you need to work on to achieve them, and the biweekly and monthly milestones. See what feels wrong and right, and revise your plan after analyzing your genuine progress and performance.

Focus on Your MITs

MIT stands for 'most important tasks,' tasks that need your attention and directly relate to your goals.

If you plan on staying hydrated, drinking ten glasses of water is your MIT related to that task.

If you have to turn in a project report due in two days, working on gathering the data and preparing the report are your MITs for that objective.

To get anything done, you must start with your MITs.

- Go through your weekly and monthly plans.

- Analyze the goals you want to achieve regarding the habits you would like to build and any other important targets.

- Figure out the MITs related to those habits and goals.

- Begin by working on them first.

If you do that right, you will achieve significant progress while keeping procrastination at bay.

Use the 80/ 20 Rule

Also known as the 'Pareto Principle,' the 80/20 rule is a famous principle that describes how 80% of the output in almost everything comes from 20% of effort invested in the right area.

According to the rule, it is mostly 20% of your effort in the most critical areas/processes/aspects/tools, etc., that yields a whopping 80% of the total outcome, and upon identifying that 20% of the most significant area, you know exactly when and where to hit the hammer on the nail.

The 80/20 rule works remarkably well at beating procrastination. Once you know those 20% tasks that produce 80% of the desirable yield, you understand the activities you need to work on at any given time to achieve 80% of the desired results. With that knowledge, you can clear all the extra activities from your schedule and focus on only what's needed.

Here's how you can use the 80/20 rule to your advantage:

- Figure out the most pressing tasks related to the goals you wish to achieve.

- Jot down those tasks.

- Schedule them first in your daily and weekly plan.

- Also, observe your prime energy time, which is the time when your energy and enthusiasm levels are the highest, and you find it easiest to work on even the toughest of tasks. Working on essential tasks in your prime energy time is another way to leverage the 80/20 rule because you tend to work faster and more efficiently.

- When working on a specific task, brainstorm different strategies and choose one that promises the most or the best outcome. This approach allows you to maximize output by investing your time, effort, and energy in a strategy that yields the maximum return.

Once you start employing the 80/20 rule, you shall notice a marked increase in productivity. As you start working better, you will gradually find it easier to overcome the urge to procrastinate.

Eat the Ugly Frog

Eating the ugly frog is a popular way to beat procrastination. Imagine devouring a frog at the start of the day.

Of course, it is disgusting and arguably the most gruesome thing ever, but once you do it, you feel capable of handling anything because you have experienced the worst. You can experience some worse things, like someone serving you another bag of frogs, but you will have accomplished much by eating an ugly frog first thing in the morning.

Eating an ugly frog is an analogy to describe the most challenging task on your schedule, the one job that gives you the jitters, never letting you rest. It eats away at your peace and gradually diminishes your enthusiasm.

If you work on it first, even though it feels even more challenging than climbing Everest, you enjoy a good adrenaline rush. Once that big task that almost felt like the most significant roadblock ever is out of the way, you get motivated to work on your entire schedule. Because of this, it is usually best to start the day with the deadliest task on the agenda when you just cannot work on anything else.

- Identify your most challenging task.

- Break it into smaller parts.

- Get started with the first part. You can work on it for 5 minutes only.

- Keep working on it in batches of 5 minutes each, and soon you'll be done with the first fragment of it.

- Keep working on it in this manner until you have it covered.

Try this hack once, and you'll find the energy and strength to manage all your tasks on time.

Complete Quick Tasks Immediately

Specific tasks do not need that much time. Quick wins, as some may call them, are the chores and activities that bring in good productivity without demanding too much effort. If you quickly tend to these tasks, you get much done in less time.

Unfortunately, many of us avoid doing even these tasks when a massive bout of procrastination consumes us. Start working on the quick tasks immediately to avoid going into that phase.

- Identify the quick and easy tasks in your schedule. They could be calling a friend, emailing an employee, preparing a proposal, creating an email account, etc.

- Analyze those tasks and figure out one you can do right away.

- Work on that particular task instantly and see how you feel.

- You are likely to feel more motivated than before and will feel ready to work on the next set of quick tasks.

- Similarly, tend to the quick tasks as soon as you assign them to ensure you finish a good chunk of your work.

Once through with a task, update it on your calendar to keep yourself from worrying about it.

Create a Mini Habit for Challenging Tasks

'Mini habit' is a term coined by Stephen Guise. It refers to creating small habits to gradually settle into a schedule or adjust to a new habit you are trying to build. It is easier to think of researching your thesis for 5 or 10 minutes than to explore the same for 6 hours or find all the content for the literature review right away.

Challenging tasks tend to devour your motivation. To keep them from doing that, create mini habits to build a habit of doing difficult tasks.

- Analyze your challenging task and break it into different segments. For instance, if you have to prepare your MBA thesis, break the task into settling on the topic, collecting data, finalizing whether to opt for a qualitative or quantitative study, deciding on a research tool, etc.

- Take every small segment of the task and chop it into smaller bits.

- Dedicate 5 to 10 minutes to each bit of the task. If researching for your thesis is a lengthy task, conduct the research for just 10 minutes thrice a day.

- In this manner, keep building mini habits to work on the task until it becomes manageable and convenient to work on and complete gradually.

Build 'Elephant Habits' for Ongoing Projects

The 'elephant habit' approach is similar to the 'eating an ugly frog' strategy. Eating an ugly frog refers to doing a challenging task first, and a building elephant habit is an approach to working on your most demanding tasks.

How do you think one would eat an elephant if one had to? Since an elephant would make quite an enormous meal, you would eat it one bite at a time. Likewise, when tackling ongoing and essential projects, work on them one bit at a time.

The strategy discussed above, and that of copping down big habits into smaller chunks, is what you need to follow to build elephant habits.

Use Sprints to Work on Challenging Projects

Have you ever sprinted? If you have, you'd know the feeling of running crazy fast to cover a certain distance in a short time. The 'sprint approach' works similarly. It requires you to work on a difficult task while challenging yourself to complete it in a specific and small time slot.

If you have to prepare a slide deck for a presentation, balance some accounts, or edit a video but are dreading that task, give yourself an exciting challenge by attaching a time slot to that task, setting the timer, and pushing yourself to complete it timely.

Build the Discomfort Habit

Discomfort is not a bad thing. We are mainly used to doing things in our comfort zone to the extent that moving past it almost seems impossible. Now that you are all set to kick out procrastination from your life, encourage yourself to build the discomfort habit.

The habit is about nudging yourself to adjust to the idea of being uncomfortable once in a while. Growth lies outside your comfort zone. You stay on the couch for years, munching on crisps and fried food, watching as your bulging belly grows, or you can get up, move around, work out and build an active lifestyle that helps you start shedding that extra body fat and weight. The same applies to everything else.

Success comes with growth. Growth depends on learning, unlearning, and experimentation. That is where building the discomfort habit comes in handy. Here's how you can build this habit:

- Figure out any one task you feel uncomfortable doing. Moreover, you could also pick an area you'd like to grow better at and identify any activity that makes you shrug your head in discomfort.

- Build a commitment to work in that area. Perhaps, you wish to be a successful public speaker but struggle with stage fright.

- As discussed above, create a roadmap to achieve that goal or tackle that uncomfortable task.

- Start by working on a tiny bit of a task on the roadmap and slowly build the discomfort habit.

If you keep working on this strategy, you will soon be quite comfortable with the idea of being uncomfortable.

Remove Hidden Blocks with the Awareness Habit

All of us have one or more inner obstacles that obstruct our growth. It is important to unravel those layers of darkness that keep light from flowing inside us. How best can we do that? By becoming aware of ourselves, and the hidden blocks.

- Dedicate 5 minutes of your day to self-introspection, primarily focused on the things that keep you from growing in life.

- As you identify a hidden block, ensure you write it down in your journal.

- Whenever you notice the block keeping you from moving forward, write about it.

- Figure out the best way to overcome that block.

- Work on the identified strategy by using the mini habits strategies.

With time and persistence, you will keep managing procrastination even better. The next chapter helps further strengthen your mindset by discussing habits solely focused on that in...

The Mindset Building Habit.

Chapter 14: The Mindset Building Habit

"Make no mistake about it. Bad habits are called 'bad' for a reason. They kill our productivity and creativity. They slow us down. They hold us back from achieving our goals. And they're detrimental to our health." **– John Rampton**

Have you ever wondered what role your mindset plays in your life and whether you can reshape it? Well, this chapter will give you fresh insight regarding your mental imaging and conclusions about life and how to transform it for the better.

If I show you a painting and ask you to find six faults, I am sure you will point out all six of them —and maybe more. At the same time, if I show the same painting to another person and ask that person to search for all the elements of perfection in it, he'll too manage to identify the right ones.

Like every painting with flaws and great finesse attributes, our life is also a piece of art. It depends on what you are searching for or what you choose to focus on at any moment. If you focus on the negative aspects, your life will be like a bleak portrait. It will be an endearing one if you have a positive outlook.

A positive mindset gives you hope to live, and life feels easy when you can explore different areas. Before starting this journey, it is essential to sanitize your mind first.

Brain Dump Journal

Have you ever felt overwhelmed and restless to an extent where your brain can't process anything? You get grumpy and lash out at people for no reason. When this happens, know it's time for a brain dump.

Your brain is not your hard drive; it's your processing tool. You must remove such negativity from your mind to enable proper brain function.

- Jot down likes, dislikes, achievements, reminders, rants, etc.

- Don't stress about organizing and putting margin lines.

- Do weekly brain dumps for improved results.

And you're done!

When you have de-cluttered your mind, it is time to start organizing your life, but you'll have to set a direction first.

Review Goals and Vision

Are You Sleepwalking Through Life?

Yes, this is different! You may be physically awake but mentally asleep when your body runs on auto mode and live without any life objectives. You don't know where you are heading; you are simply sleepwalking your life away.

Setting goals is essential, and so is remembering them. Like a brain dump journal, you can also make one as a vision list.

- Define a significant goal, its parameters, and requirements

- Set milestones

- Paste relatable stickers to make it inspiring and worth revisiting

- Make a rough draft for a neat final look

When "walking" through life, it is essential to be aware of your actions; otherwise, you can get carried away by the winds. Let's see how you can have a safe journey.

Become Aware of Your Actions

People often take feedback as an offense. The problem is not with the feedback. It's with "not-knowing" whom to take it from—the individual. There is a difference between constructive and destructive feedback. One builds while the other tears down!

Yes, the advice here is to ask for feedback to become aware of your actions, but people often select the wrong source of feedback. When someone mocks and calls it feedback, you automatically become defensive about those very actions you need to change.

Therefore, it's advisable to consider a mentor or a loved one for this. They provide constructive feedback, making you feel respected and willing to alter your behavior.

You will also become watchful of your actions and have positive feedback in the end.

Take this as your first challenge if you think it's hard.

Let's see how to learn and implement this...

Take on the challenge

The easiest way to face a challenge is to run right into it. When you accept a challenge, you become familiar with it, making it look easy. Meanwhile, not failing gives you confidence that you can succeed if you put in a little extra effort.

For any challenge in life:

- Write down what scares you as a brain dump

- Know that others face it too

- Ask for guidance from an experienced person

- Set self-treats

- Revisit your vision list

Once you have mastered the art, the new challenges will seem like a cake unless you are distracted.

Now let's discuss how to control distractions...

Block Out Your Schedule

You get easily distracted when you don't have time pressure and know you can drag your task to as many days as possible. The way out is to set small goals daily and time them.

- Divide a primary objective into smaller goals

- Set daily targets

- Score your performance

- Take a day off to refresh and fulfill your cravings

- Set penalties for extra work when you miss deadlines

Distractions aren't the only factor that disrupts the growth of a mindset. Sometimes, other elements come in the way.

Let's look at how you can maintain a growth-oriented mindset!

Mindset Check-Ins

Maintaining a growth mindset is an ongoing process that requires constant attention, and if you fail to check yourself regularly, you will shift back to a fixed mindset. Whenever you think you can't manage to move forward, know that you are reverting to your old self. If you continue to stick there, you will lose all progress.

To cultivate a growth mindset, you should:

- Accept that you are unbeatable. (The more challenges you take on, the better)

- Don't seek external approval. (With practice, you'll know it's not hard)

- Pen down self-doubt, self-imposed limits, external restrictions, etc., as part of your brain dump.

- Be open to new experiences. (It will be hard in the start if you are not used to it, but with time, you'll get comfortable)

Failure often leads you to a fixed mindset, but no one can avoid disappointment, right?

Then, what's the way out?

Failure Isn't the End; It's a New Beginning

You can't escape failure, but you can give it a new definition. This time you have learned the best experience and are not starting from scratch. Every time you fail, your chances of success increase.

Every time you fail, you get a step closer to your goal. Every time you fail, it adds to your skill and knowledge. Every time you fail, you get more insight into defining your purpose. Viewing failure as a new start is the key to success.

"Every new beginning comes from some other beginning's end."

Seneca

Once you have built a positive mindset, you are ready to work on the next set of habits that revolve around setting your daily goals.

Chapter 15: The Daily Goal Setting Habit

"If you're bored with life – you don't get up every morning with a burning desire to do things – you don't have enough goals." — **Lou Holtz**

The quote above clearly shows how goals add value and meaning to our life. If you often feel bored, like your life lacks meaning, it is time to enrich it with some powerful and substantial goals. We have the perfect remedy for you

This chapter focuses on helping you set the habit of building daily goals.

Set Goals in Advance

Planning is certainly time-consuming. Just like you are supposed to plan your day ahead of time, you should similarly work on your goals. Instead of setting up your daily goals on that very day, think of what you would like to accomplish the next day the night before.

- Ensure you write down your targets for the next day so that you are all set to work on them the next day.

- When setting a goal, ensure it means something to you.

- Write down the compelling whys pegged to that goal. If you want to create a course module on e-commerce, why do you want to do that?

- Attach a starting and ending date to your goal to ensure you know when to get started with it and when it will be due.

Read your goal out aloud to solidify your commitment to it.

Break Down Your Long-Term Goals

When a goal is too big, it scares you to the core. The idea of losing 40 pounds may sound intimidating, but the instant you think of losing a pound or two a month, it stops feeling all that frightening, right? That's the power of breaking your long-term goals into smaller bits and pieces.

- Take your long-term goal, and break it into mid-term and short-term milestones.

- If your long-term goal spreads over 2 years, have a mid-term milestone at the end of the first year, with the short-term goals spread over 6 months.

- Once you have clear medium-term and short-term goals, take the short-term goals and break them down into actionable steps. These are the activities you need to do every day to accomplish the target and then move toward the mid-term goal.

- Sew in all the activities, and you have your action plan ready.

- Revisit it regularly, say at least every two weeks, to ensure you keep heading in the right direction.

3 Goals per-Day

Work on no more than 3 goals per day related to different activities of your life. Here, the term goals refer to your daily targets. For instance, your health-related goal could be to work out in the gym for 30 minutes, your work-related goal could be to design a branding strategy for your client, and your personal goal could be to get a massage.

Do not fill your plate with too many daily targets because that can be exhausting. Instead, work on any 3 important targets, and strive to achieve them with excellence.

Be Consistent

Once you have an action plan, even if you are unsure of the plan but at least have a goal set in mind, work on it consistently. Consistency is the golden rule for success in every endeavor. If you take consistent action daily, you will eventually reach the finish line, even with a hundred failed attempts.

Every day, you must take some action, even if it is a tiny step towards your goal. Keep track of your performance and keep building on it daily.

Focus on Action, Not Planning

Planning is great, but taking action is even more important. Do not spend hours planning, exhausting yourself to a point where you cannot take action anymore. Instead, plan for a bit and save your energy to walk the walk.

Figure out the starting point, and then act on it. Taking action right away helps you get in the groove. Once you keep taking steps, you build momentum and gain pace.

Stay Accountable

Accountability is a crucial virtue that helps you stick to what you believe in, take stock of your performance, and improve it. Once you start working on a goal, take complete responsibility for it.

- Set an intention to achieve your goal.

- Conduct daily check-ins with your feelings about the goal.

- Chant your intention to work on the goal.

- Assess your performance through and through.

- Accept when you falter and miss a step. Perhaps, you could not work on adding more content to your YouTube channel for a week. Acknowledge the slip-up and improvise the strategy to work on the target.

- Acknowledge your strengths and appreciate your efforts. Find ways to leverage them and keep moving efficiently towards your objectives.

- You can also have an accountability partner to ensure you responsibly work on your targets. Ask a friend to check your performance and remind you of your deliverables and milestones timely.

Most Important First

Never underestimate the importance of high-priority tasks. They are the activities that accelerate your progress. Hence, it makes sense to put them first, always. Take stock of your high-priority tasks at night when planning for the next day, and dive right into them the next morning.

As you work on these habits, carve out some time from your routine to work on building the reading habit. It is one habit that goes a long way.

The Reading Habit

"The more you read, the more you know. The more you know, the more places you go." — **Dr. Seuss**

If reading is your superpower, there is nothing that can stop you from being magical. Reading more helps you learn more, broadens your horizons, awakens your intuitive and imaginative capabilities, improves your knowledge and awareness, and helps you do things better.

You don't need to begin by reading 500-page books every day; you only need to start small. Like all the other habits we have discussed before, reading is a habit you can build very easily with the help of micro habits.

- Pick any genre of content you enjoy. It could be suspense, drama, thriller, romance, fantasy — whatever you please.

- Choose the fiction or non-fiction category.

- After deciding what you want to read, search for a few bestsellers or interesting books.

- Go for paper-back editions if you don't feel like spending money on a hardcover book. You can also borrow a book from a friend or go for an eBook or PDF version of the book you want to read.

- Read five pages of your favorite book every morning.

- You could stack up this habit on top of an already built habit or one that you are now more used to —say, journaling, or, if you now have a habit of meditating daily, perhaps you could read a page of your current book then.

- If reading even a page seems a bit too much, read a paragraph, but ensure you do something every day!

Remember what Lao Tzu said: *'The journey of a thousand miles begins with a single step.'*

I want you to hold on tightly to this thought and practice it in your daily routine. Reading daily is a blessing; you will start reaping its magic once you get on with it.

Performing Strategy (Habit Stacking)

As has been the case with all the habits we have discussed in the previous parts, let us get moving with the performing strategy for the mindset habits too.

Duration: Set a fixed time to work on all the mindset habits. If you have decided to practice the elephant habit approach for 5 minutes, stick to it. Try not to lengthen it to 10 minutes or shorten it to 2 minutes. Stick to 5 minutes for two weeks, and gradually build on it. If 5 minutes feels long on the first day, cut back on the duration of the respective habit, and stick to it for two weeks.

Best time: Observe yourself as you engage in a particular habit at different times to find the time that works best for you. This can take some time, usually 5 to 10 days. Be patient with yourself during this period. Once you identify the best time, only work on that habit at that particular time of the day.

Important insights: Watch yourself engage in the habit very calmly and nonjudgmentally. See how you work on it when you are well-rested or on days when you are sleep-deprived. Take stock of how your mood on different days affects your performance and how you work on managing it.

How to Perform: Try working on a certain habit in different ways. Perhaps you could read while traveling on the bus one day and then read in a library the next day. You could play some music while reading and then try without it. Experiment with different ideas while working on a habit to figure out the best strategy to perform it.

Strategy to Practice the Mindset Habits Together

When you sew together different habits, you create a sequence of powerful habits that lift one another. Here's a strategy to practice the different mindset habits we have discussed in this part of the book as a whole:

- Go over your plan for the day that you made the night before.

- Review your goals and chant your vision statement to take stock of it.

- Revisit your 3 goals for the day.

- Have a mindset check-in for 2 minutes.

- Check for any emergency that may have popped up or is stirring up and tackle it.

- Work on any quick task right away.

- See if there is a deadly task you need to work on using the 'eat the frog strategy.'

- Tackle the bigger projects using the 'elephant habit' approach.

- Keep working on the rest of your tasks for the day with the combination of 'mini habit' and 'sprint' techniques.

- Read a passage or two of any books you are reading currently.

This is a straightforward way to combine the different mindset habits to turn them into lifelong habits that stick with you for the long haul.

Part 5:
Productivity and
Workflow Habits

"In essence, if we want to direct our lives, we must take control of our consistent actions. It's not what we do that shapes our lives, but what we do consistently."

— **Tony Robbins**

Chapter 16: The Focus Habit

"Only through focus can you do world-class things, no matter how capable you are." — **Bill Gates**

From classmates and colleagues to friends and family members, we all know people who always complete their work before the due date. They know what to do to complete their work almost half the time required by an average person. They are normal human beings, just like you and me. What sets them apart from the rest is their productivity habits.

Productivity habits, as the name states, are those habits that allow you to be efficient and productive in your work and duties, and in your professional and personal life. Productivity habits will enable you to overcome challenges like procrastination, laziness, boredom, distractions, and demotivation. By developing productive habits, you can be efficient in all your tasks and have a better productivity rate.

Staying focused is no easy task, especially during stressful days that require you to attend to cumbersome tasks. Distractions can take many forms and invade our minds anytime we try to concentrate on our work. This chapter will emphasize one thing: habits can allow you to maintain focus.

To be productive, remember that it starts from being focused. In simpler terms, the ability to focus means paying attention to a specific task or thought, for a particular amount of time, without getting distracted.

Below are some of the habits that have helped me maintain focus.

Being compassionate

Compassion means recognizing the pain and suffering of the people around you and helping them in any way you can. Being compassionate makes you more aware of your surroundings. When compassionate towards someone, you tend to focus on their behavior and moods and analyze how you could help the distressed person.

There are four steps involved in being compassionate effectively.

- The "cognitive" step means creating awareness and attention about suffering in the first place.

- Secondly, the "effective" part focuses on the emotional effect felt after seeing another person suffering.

- Thirdly, the "intentional" part is where you wish to do something about the suffering and end it.

- Lastly, the "motivation" component is where you are ready to take action to end the suffering.

Focus at will

Focusing on your work is no easy task, especially with the many distractions in our modern environments. Studies show that social media, news, gossip, and a noisy atmosphere are the leading causes of distractions.

- Firstly, create a work schedule and follow it to the dot. After making a routine schedule, follow it. Placing time limits on your work is an effective way of following the program without being distracted.

- Secondly, turn off your phone notifications. Calls, social media notifications, and news pings often distract us from our tasks, causing focus losses. Turning off the volume is a more straightforward way of maintaining the created focus.

- Lastly, take short breaks in between your tasks to maintain your focus.

Avoid multitasking

Multitasking distracts us from the critical tasks at hand and leads to a steady drop in our focus.

One of the most effective ways to decrease multitasking is clearing your line of sight of anything irrelevant in front of you. If you're working on your desktop, ensure only the task you are currently working on is before you, not the next.

Learning to say "no" is another way to stop multitasking. Your primary focus should be your tasks. Plus, when working on a job, fully involve yourself by concentrating on the little steps.

Disconnection habits

Disconnection habits help us focus better on our tasks and goals by cutting off or "disconnecting" ourselves from distractions. Working in silence and calming atmosphere is a peaceful way to disconnect from distractions.

Social media is one of the major causes of distractions these days. Once you open the app, you waste precious time without realizing how much time has passed. Disconnecting from social media and news while working is quite productive as it leads to less inefficiency and makes the task easier.

Inform coworkers and colleagues beforehand not to disturb you during work hours, as it can become quite distracting and lead to time-wasting.

Take breaks

All work and no play make Jack a dull boy. Working the entire day with no other activities or breaks is stressful and leads to inefficiency and less productivity.

Taking short breaks between work lets you relax and de-stress. During these breaks, talk to your coworkers about non-work-related topics, listen to light music, and rest your eyes for a minute or two.

Go for a walk outside your office in nature. Having some fresh air refreshes you and makes your day more productive. Drink a cool glass of water to de-stress yourself.

Stretch your muscles, most notably the shoulders. Sitting in a single position during work hours creates tension in your shoulders and back.

While working on these habits, also try to do a task single-handedly. This is an effective hack to maintain killer focus. Let's talk about it next.

Chapter 17: The Single Tasking Habit

"At any moment in the day, you can only do one thing at a time. And the more intentional you are about knowing what your #1 is, the more present you will be." — **Rob Bell**

Single-tasking, also called monotasking, is the opposite of multitasking. It involves being wholly focused on a single task, thus ensuring you put everything else on hold until the current task is complete.

Monotasking is highly efficient and productive as it keeps you focused on a single task without any distractions or side tasks that can lead to inefficiency.

Remember, single-tasking is all about professional workplaces and educational institutes. It is also a central practice with friends and loved ones in your personal life. When you give time to your family, ensure you are not thinking about or focused on work. Instead, give your family the full attention they deserve.

Some of the most commonly used ways to increase single-tasking are:

Decide to Do One Thing At a Time

One of the main reasons we multitask is that we cannot decide what task to prioritize and focus on first. Instead, we combine them and take on all of them.

To avoid multitasking, you should always look into your plans and schedules for tasks and goals. Prioritize your tasks by numbering and ranking them, probably from highest to lowest.

You will have to convince yourself to focus on just one task at a time and work on that. One of the tricks to focus more on the task is to say it aloud and emphasize, "Yes, I have to focus on just task A and complete that."

Visualize Yourself Doing that Task

This strategy involves imagery and imagination that help you visualize how you will perform the chosen task and how you plan to achieve it.

After visualizing the task, close your eyes and relax. Envision yourself preparing for the job, starting from scratch and basic steps, moving on to the complex ones, and finishing them successfully.

Say No to Your Urges and Temptations

Distractions exist all around us, more so when we are trying to focus on our work. A coworker coming to talk, your mobile phone ringing, and a knock on the door are some actions that break our concentration and focus level.

With a solid and focused mind, telling yourself to concentrate verbally is also a great way to say no to urges. Telling yourself "No" when avoiding distractions out loud is crucial to keeping your focus intact at times.

Focus on the End Result

When focused on a task, always remember what's important here: **the result.**

When you know the result you experience after completing a task, you will remain focused and motivated to work more efficiently on the given task. Think of why you are working on something, why a specific goal means so much, and why you must achieve a target. Think of reaching the finish line; you'll get enough motivation to do it.

Reward Yourself

After completing your task and getting the expected result, it is time to relax and take a break.

If you are at work, put on some light music, scroll through your social media feed, or watch an analysis of the football match you chose to miss to complete your work. If you are home, treat yourself to a hot meal, some movie or TV show you like, and some quiet and peace.

Block Time for longer tasks

Time blocking is a technique that divides your day into smaller blocks of time. In each block, you perform a specific activity/task. With time blocking, you waste less on deciding what to focus on since you have a prepared schedule.

Since time blocking builds on single-tasking, it can improve your productivity by 80%, which is not something we can say about multitasking.

When you schedule every moment of your day, you increase your focus on each task you need to complete to achieve your milestones.

Time blocks work best for priority tasks that need more time. Blocking time also works well for small breaks throughout the day.

With that covered, let's move to the next set of habits to help increase your productivity.

Chapter 18: The Learning Habit

"I am always ready to learn, although I do not always like being taught." — **Winston Churchill**

You never stop learning, whether a high school student or working a full-time professional job.

You do not wake up one day and decide that you have mastered the art of coding, for example. Learning starts with small continuous steps practiced daily for something to become a habit. That is why you need to build the habit of learning to keep growing better.

The habit of learning allows us to have a more open mindset. This allows us to be a better version of ourselves by constantly learning. Learning continuously will enable us to remain valuable and maintain our expertise level.

Despite our willingness to learn, hectic college and office work demands hardly leave us with any free time to make a habit of learning something new.

You can develop the habit of learning effectively by engaging in the following micro habits:

Set a learning period in your daily goals list

If you have made a list of the achievement you want to achieve to attain your daily goals, you should add another one with the heading "learning skill."

Pick up any skill you have always wanted to learn. The first step in every learning is the intention to do it. Knowledge is only effective if your mind and body are ready for it.

Once you have made up your mind, deciding the appropriate time to learn and practice is the next major step. For example, some learning tasks, like learning a new language, take up to an hour of daily routine. However, some minor skills can take up to 20-30 minutes of your time, which is easy to do.

Dedicating that time to learning something new daily allows your learning to be effective. As you know, avoid any gaps or distractions as they hurt our learning habits.

Create a weekly learning planner of things you want to learn for the next seven days

Now that you have chosen a skill, it is time to schedule the components you have to practice to learn effectively.

If we talk about learning a **new cooking recipe**, the first stage is to gather all the ingredients. A pizza, for example, would require dough, yeast, cheese, tomatoes, etc., as ingredients. An oven in which to bake it is another requirement.

Getting the ingredients in the correct quantity is one of the most crucial parts of learning a new recipe. The mixing, resting and cooking all follow it.

Do not be disheartened if you get it wrong the first time. As cliché as it sounds, failure is always a primary key to success.

Writing a blog

Blogging has gone quite mainstream in the last decade now. Writing a blog is more about getting the right audience than writing an article. Before you start writing, you must know the audience you have chosen to target. Is this audience ready to see the different sides of the story? Will it resonate with them?

Due to the immense saturation in the blogging community, it is best to start by figuring out your competitors. Knowing your competitor is worth it, as you can analyze the strategies and angles by which they have captivated their audiences.

Choosing the topics to cover would be demanding as you have information readily available on the internet and news channels. Choosing a unique and different case is the challenge most writers face.

After meeting all the prerequisites, the final task is to start writing. Would you be writing professionally, formally, or informally? Would you be using British English or American? Deciding these points before every article is of the utmost importance for a blog writer.

When it comes to learning a new exercise, the first step is approaching your trainer. Since workouts significantly impact your body, you should perform them with great precision.

After talking with your trainer about it, watching videos about the exercise would help as they show different angles and techniques to practice and learn the workout.

Working out five days a week would be enough to learn and perfect the new workout. Practicing a new movement would take about 10-15 minutes of your total workout time.

However, learning a new language would take more time than other skills. Learning a new language takes around 12 to 18 months.

Fortunately, many options are now available for learning a new language. Today, you can find online courses, mobile phone applications, school courses, and books that teach you a specific language.

The first thing to keep in mind while learning a new language is setting goals because it will be difficult to measure your success level if you don't. These goal settings include, for example, the Turkish language alphabet you have to learn this week.

To learn a new language, one must always start with the alphabet, colloquialisms, and essential words before moving on to sentences and proper reading.

Similarly, whatever you decide to learn, start from scratch and slowly climb up the ladder.

Part 6: Wealth Habits

Chapter 19: The De-cluttering Habit

"The first step in crafting the life you want is to get rid of everything you don't." — **Joshua Becker**

Cluttering happens when we become too stressed at work or too lazy to clean our space. We keep stacking books, papers, and useless documents in a pile until it's nearly impossible to locate a helpful document at the right time.

De-cluttering simply means removing unnecessary items from your desk or workplace, thus making our workplace look tidy and professional. Decluttering also has countless other benefits that we will talk about below.

Clutter leads to disorganization, which can cause feelings of "being out of control in life." Clutter can also affect your physical health, as piles of items invite much dust, often leading to dust allergies or worse conditions.

On the other hand, de-cluttering helps build your confidence and self-esteem by organizing your life in small, necessary steps. Since everything is organized and kept in its proper place, dusty items' chances are slim.

Let us now look at the habits you can build to start de-cluttering.

One in, One out

This is probably one of the most uncommon but helpful decluttering tips. It's simple: whenever you bring something new home, give away the old one.

As harsh as it sounds, it does not mean giving away prized possessions. We have countless articles of clothing in our wardrobes that we have not even looked at in ages, yet they sit there collecting dust. Giving them away while getting a new one would benefit your storage space.

To give away something you have had for a long time, you have to convince yourself, "Yes, I am doing the right thing. I honestly do not need it anymore". Afterward, go through the clutter and pick out the items you have not used recently or, let's say, the past half-year. You put them in a bag and get rid of them.

Attack Clutter 15 Minutes a Day, six days a Week

When you finally decide that the clutter on your desk makes work difficult, it's time to attack it with a relaxed and calm head. It's important to know that not everything should go into the trash. There might be some important documents and items you need in the future.

To clear clutter efficiently, attack it for not more than 15 minutes a day. Thoroughly check which documents you can shred and which ones you still need.

Toss Some Items A Day, 6 Days A Week

After keeping the essential items aside, for example, your clothes, it's time to get rid of the old ones.

We usually have piles of clothes we do not need anymore. We might have outgrown them, or they are out of fashion now. Either way, it is time to get rid of them.

However, getting rid of something does not mean throwing it away in the trash. You can donate things you do not need. You can use old clothes to make dusting clothes or use them in other productive ways, such as to learn sewing. On the other hand, place any document not needed in the office anymore in its folder or shred it.

Every Weekend Attack One Clutter Pile Until it is Gone

De-cluttering during the weekdays might seem a mighty task, even though it seems small and manageable. At home, we have countless piles of clutter. Probably one for every room and those of every kind. Clothes, books, papers, stationery, kitchen items, etc.

Make some time over the weekends to de-clutter one pile at a time. Start with the ones that take the shortest time. Accomplishing this task would motivate you to do more on the coming weekend, and before you know it, your place will be clutter-free.

Tidy Up For 15 Minutes After Dinner

After eating your dinner, do not hit the couch just yet. You can be just a little more productive before retiring for the day.

As tiring as it sounds, try to de-clutter right after your dinner. Pick the most accessible pile to de-clutter and sort it out for no more than 15 minutes. Doing this would give you a sense of accomplishment at the end of the day, and your workload for the coming day and weekend would reduce by one pile.

Never Leave a Room Empty-Handed

One basic rule that can help with de-cluttering is never leaving a room empty-handed. Consistently taking things out of the room back to where they belong is a good way of ensuring clutter does not pile up again.

Picking up an item or two from, let's suppose, your dining room and moving it back to the kitchen on your way there is both efficient and helpful. When heading to your room from the kitchen, pick up your watch and take it back to your room.

This habit does not come naturally to some and may take time to form. Only patience and determination to not leave the room empty-handed will help make this habit permanent.

Put Stuff Back the Moment You Are Finished Using It

After using an item, please do not leave it lying around. It would only give you an excuse to put other things there when you are done with them, leading to a mess and clutter in no time.

Immediately after using something, put the thing back right where it belongs. For example, putting the phone charger back in its usual place will help you locate it quickly the next time you need it. There would not be clutter because everything would be in its designated place.

Set a Regular Donation Goal

After deciding to de-clutter the pile in your room, put the items to give away in boxes and trash bags.

After clearing out more of the clutter every weekend, make a trip to the donation center and give away all the unnecessary items you have cleared out that can still be useful to others.

Decluttering in this way is a quick and easy method to get rid of your old stuff productively. It also makes you happy to see that other people appreciate the things you and your family do not use anymore.

You create space for things you genuinely like as you eliminate unwanted, used, old, and meaningless stuff from your home. Plus, decluttering in this way also decreases your mental clutter and stress. As a result, you find it easier to focus on ideas, prospects, and activities that help you grow your wealth.

Chapter 20: The Money Budgeting Habit (Tracking Expenses)

"If you are going to achieve excellence in big things, you develop the habit in little matters. Excellence is not an exception, it is a prevailing attitude." — **Colin Powell**

You don't get wealthier by thinking of having more money. Building budgeting habits are among the many ways to keep growing richer with time. Budgeting allows you to spend your money wisely, manage your expenses, and increase your savings. You later need to invest those savings in some profitable business or income source to continue multiplying your money.

Budgeting may seem like an uphill task, but we have some mini habits to help you stop living from one paycheck to another.

Create a Monthly Money Budget

You wouldn't know how much you should spend and how much you can reasonably splurge if you don't have a budget. Budgeting helps you understand the financial boundaries you must and must not cross.

- Begin by assessing your basic needs and absolute necessities.

- Put down staples and necessities like groceries, utilities, bills, rent, and other essential expenses you have every month, and those you cannot make do without at all costs.

- Set aside a flexibility room for about $100, $300, or $500 for any contingency.

- Add up the numbers. That final count is your must-do expenses.

- Set up a monthly budget to cover that amount.

Keep Tracking Your Expenditure

As the month starts and moves by, track your expenses.

- Divide the monthly budget into a weekly budget.

- Every week, there should be a certain amount of money you can spend.

- Keep a check on that number by observing your daily and weekly expenses.

Find Ways to Reduce Your Expenses

Being creative with managing your funds isn't as hard as it seems. As essential as the basic expenses are, you can still find ways to reduce them.

Here are some ideas that can help you out:

- Create a 'dollar jar,' and throw a dollar in it daily. It doesn't seem easy to put aside $100 right away, but if you keep tossing in a dollar each day in the jar, you'll have $100 saved in less than four months. Not a bad idea at all, right?

- Buy commonly used items like staple foods, groceries, and household utilities in bulk. Instead of buying one toilet paper roll, purchase a pack of 6. You'll save some bucks and a whole lot of effort.

- Turn off extra lights in the rooms, and avoid leaving the tap running when you're not using it. These good hacks conserve energy and lower your bills quite a bit.

- Avoid ordering food often and prepare meals at home. Home-cooked meals are healthier and also easier on the pocket.

- Every time you get an urge to splurge on something pricey, put that money aside. Say you had an eye for a pair of sunglasses at the mall worth $150. If you weren't on a budget, you might have bought those. So why not put that $150 aside and save it now?

Similarly, look for exciting ways to save a few to a couple of hundred dollars every month. Setting saving goals can prove massively helpful.

Set Savings Goals from the Budget

Like all the other habits, you can achieve something when you set a clear goal centered on it. Set some saving goals from your budget to start saving like a pro.

- Think of an amount you'd like to save from your budget.

- It is best to have an exact amount instead of being vague and thinking, "I'd like to save a couple of hundred dollars." Reflect on your budget and how much you think you can save comfortably, and put that number down.

- Create an intention centered on that amount. The choice should be concise, positive, and present-oriented. For instance, you can say, "I am saving $200 in May 2022." This clear goal is quite positive and states that you are working on saving money. The human mind accepts what you feed it; if you tell it you are saving money in the present moment now, it believes it.

As you start saving more, your wealth will grow gradually, giving you much financial freedom.

High-Performance Engagement Habit

*"You are the average of the five people you spend the most time with." — **Jim Rohn***

The people you surround yourself with impact your attitude, behavior, and lifestyle. If you spend time around a fitness enthusiast for two weeks, you may not get six packs right away, but you will find the zeal to hit the gym more.

Thus, to become more productive and achieve your goals, you need to build a 'high-performance engagement' habit. This refers to spending more time with high-level performers who keep achieving or have achieved what you want in life.

- To become wealthier, figure out some rich and influential people in your social circle.

- Spend some time thinking of how you wish to interact with those people and the kind of bond you want with them. Once you have figured that out, reach out to those people.

- When spending time out with them, ask them questions about what you want in life and any wealth-related queries you have. If you have trouble making money through your marketing agency, get in touch with a marketing specialist and ask the person about how to fill in the gaps.

- Be open to suggestions and input from the high performers in your social circle.

- As you get more feedback and ideas from them, implement them. Only by trying new things can you start getting results.

One advice many high performers, especially the wealthy, often give is to reinvest your money into a profitable business or income stream. You need to build this habit now that you want to grow wealthier—and have some savings.

Invest & Reinvest Your Funds

Money does not grow on its own. You make it grow. To develop a seed into a plant, you nourish it. Similarly, you need to grow your money if you wish to multiply it by manifolds by investing and reinvesting your funds into different investment options.

It is essential to have a diversified portfolio comprising investments in stocks, bonds, businesses, real estate, different financial tools, etc. Of course, it is best to start small, but it is crucial to take that first step. As you start saving more, invest 10% of your funds every month in some sort of investment to gradually grow your money.

Performing Strategy

With wealth habits, you also need to pay attention to the duration, best time, important insights, and the performing strategy to determine the best way to engage in those practices.

To help you build long-term habits, here's a strategy you can use to combine the wealth habits discussed in this part of the book.

- Start your day by de-cluttering your dining table or kitchen. Spend no more than 5 minutes doing that.

- Go through your monthly and weekly budgets for the day.

- See where to invest some of your funds.

- Take a 10-minute de-cluttering break to toss out some useless items at the end of the day.

- Analyze your savings and investment projects before hitting the bed at the end of the day.

With your wealth goals getting back on track, in the next section, let's focus on your...

Habits for Personal Growth.

Part 7: Habits for Personal Growth

"You'll never change your life until you change something you do daily. The secret of your success is found in your daily routine."

– John C. Maxwell

Habits for Personal Growth: Introduction

"If your compassion does not include yourself, it is incomplete." — **Jack Kornfield**

Being compassionate to others is something we all try to do. In that process, we often forget to be kind to ourselves. Your personal growth depends on being friendly, kind, and respectful to yourself.

Personal growth is about self-development and self-improvement. You need to work on your personality to achieve your goals, be financially successful, continuously climb the success ladder, and be the most refined version of yourself.

A lazy, emotionally weak, scared, and stressed-out individual who lacks self-belief will struggle to set goals and actualize them. On the other hand, strong, confident, courageous, and positive people will find it easier to objectify their aims because they are a go-getter. This attitude does not just come on its own. Yes, you pick it from your environment, but you can also sculpt it yourself. Habits revolving around personal growth are what help you construct these virtues.

Let us talk more about those habits in this part of the book.

Chapter 21: The Self-Care Habit

"Forget inspiration. Habit is more dependable. Habit will sustain you whether you're inspired or not."
– Octavia Butler

Self-care is about looking after your health and well-being. We have discussed some vital self-care habits in an earlier part of the book. Since we are diving into personal growth right now, it makes sense to talk about self-care once more from a different angle.

Many of us are so used to not looking after ourselves. We keep forgetting our own needs, health, well-being, and development. Because of this, it is important to stress the importance of self-care habits.

A tired body and mind cannot run the extra mile. Similarly, when you haven't cared for your soul for the longest time, you lose the zeal and zest to strive for betterment in life.

Let us change that for the better today. Let us start caring more for ourselves. Let us work on our confidence and well-being. Let us build the self-care habits that help us achieve these goals.

Go for a Run or a Light Jog

Exercise promotes the production of mood-improving hormones such as dopamine and serotonin in your body that lifts your spirits. Every day, or if not seven days a week, then at least 3 to 5 days a week, dedicate 10 to 15 minutes to a light jog or run. Hit the streets, run around the block, and let the fresh air engulf you in its calmness.

Take a Break When You Need it

We keep working hard and then work some more. Amidst this process, we forget that we need a break every once in a while. You have learned how to meditate and take mindset check-ins. These habits help you tune into your feelings and take stock of your emotions.

When you feel swamped and need a break, go ahead and take it. Do not question your need to relax for even one bit. Go rest for an hour, have a 40-minute nap, and stop working on the computer when your mind feels chaotic. Rejuvenate your spirits by giving yourself a break; you deserve it.

Find Out What You Love

We looked at thinking deeply, knowing ourselves, and spending time with ourselves. Those habits help you figure out what you love and are passionate about in life. Keep making journal entries about what you enjoy doing, ideas you are excited about, and everything you love, then *put that information to good use.

Every day, dedicate at least 30 minutes, if not more, to the things you love. You could dance, listen to your favorite songs, cook, or cycle around the block. Additionally, have weekly rituals revolving around yourself. For instance, Fridays can be 'spa days,' Saturdays can be 'Zumba days,' and Mondays can be about baking buns with friends.

Choose Whom You Spend Time with

This is a continuation of the 'spending time with high performers' habit discussed in the last part of the book. When deciding which people to spend time with, choose the positive, happy, supportive, and compassionate lot. Be with those who build you up, not those who find ways to break you down.

Laugh Heartily At Least Once a Day

A hearty laugh makes you forget your woes. It warms up your heart and soul and brightens the people around you. Every day, dedicate a few seconds to minutes to laughing openly and heartily only for yourself.

Think of a funny memory from your past, watch a stand-up comedy clip, talk to an entertaining friend, or force yourself to laugh for no reason at all if nothing works. This practice may seem strange initially, but you'll feel an inner light and calm once you do it. With time, and as you do it more, you will notice your stress levels reducing by manifolds, which will help you work harder and better.

Eat Green Daily

Green veggies and fruits contain antioxidants, minerals, vitamins, fiber, and other healthy elements that keep you agile, strong, healthy, and vibrant. Add a fresh, green vegetable or two to your diet daily. Stock up on cucumbers, capsicums, bean sprouts, kale, spinach, apples, and green fruits and vegetables. You can make salads out of them, prepare smoothies, sauté them, have them as sides with steaks and rice, or just eat them raw.

Avoid Emotional Eating

A lot of us are guilty of stress eating. When something goes wrong, we try to shove that terrible feeling down with cake, pizza, and more food, many of which are junk and processed.

Hey, it is okay to be in that spot once in a while. We have all had days of stress eating, and there's no need to beat yourself up. That said, emotional eating should only be a rare occurrence in your life. Making it a norm upsets your gut, makes you unhealthy, creates weight management issues, and imbalances your cholesterol levels.

To avoid emotional eating, here's what you can do:

- Practice deep breathing every time you feel a bout of intense emotions taking over you.

- Drink cool water to calm down your anger and stress.

- Go out for a quick stroll when you feel emotionally distressed.

- Tune into your emotions, and talk yourself out of the bad feeling by giving yourself positive suggestions.

- Talk to a helpful friend who can help you feel better.

- Watch something uplifting, funny, and happy.

- If you feel like eating something when stressed, have some dark chocolate at home, and take a bite of it when the ideas we have discussed cannot help you manage your stress. Dark chocolate is rich in protein, dietary fiber, iron, magnesium, and carbs. It is suitable for your health and mental well-being and eating a bit of it every day won't harm your health.

Start working on these ideas, and keep telling yourself that you are calm, happy, and have your emotions under control.

Set Boundaries with Technology and Media

Technology is excellent, and social media is very entertaining and helpful. However, too much of everything is never healthy. Long hours spent using digital technologies and surfing social media affect your productivity, focus, and performance at work. Additionally, the blue rays emitted by screens disturb your circadian rhythm (the internal body clock that regulates your sleep and other bodily functions), leading to poor sleep issues.

What should you do? Start setting boundaries with technology and media:

- Switch off notifications for social media apps to ensure you don't get repeatedly pulled toward them.

- Only check your phone in the morning to switch off alarms, set new reminders if needed, and check your daily plan if you note it on your phone.

- Set aside 10-minutes in your day to check messages, calls, and emails and respond to them. You can have two to three of these periods during the day.

- Use social media, apps, and similar websites/apps for only 30 minutes twice daily. When you set a time limit to use social media, check emails, etc., stick to this time religiously.

- Ditch your phone, laptop, and other gadgets at home and with loved ones.

Like with other habits, set reminders to stick to these practices.

Start a Journal

Various passages in this book have asked you to jot down your progress in a journal. If you have already started doing that, you have a journal. It is now time to continue and turn it into a lifelong practice.

Having a journal with multiple sections you can dedicate to different areas of your life is best. Note down the habits related to every area and your progress in it.

Develop a Daily Self-care Routine

Self-care should be a daily practice, and not just a weekly, bi-monthly, monthly, or even yearly event. It is about caring for yourself and ensuring you stay healthy and happy. Here's an idea for a self-care routine that can help you:

- Take a shower early morning.

- Dress well and put on your best clothes.

- Make sure to have a healthy breakfast.

- Keep some healthy snacks with you, such as fruit, salads, nuts, and seeds that you can munch on during the day.

- Moisturize your skin daily—this goes for guys too.

- Work out during the day.

- Make a DIY face scrub and apply it to your face before bedtime.

- When you return home from work, take a shower to unwind and soothe your stressed nerves.

As weekly rituals, you can add massages, spa days, manicures, pedicures, and other self-care regimens to this routine.

As you work on grooming yourself, you will find it easier to believe in yourself, thereby shaping your confidence. The next chapter shares with you more mini habits for building your self-belief.

Chapter 22: The Confidence Habit

"Your success will be determined by your confidence and fortitude." — **Michelle Obama**

Your confidence is the best ornament you can ever wear. The glow and elegance it adds to your personality are purely magical. It shapes how you carry yourself, interact with others, and present yourself to others. The more confident you are and behave, the more you draw others towards you. Your confidence makes you a magnet for others and plays a huge role in your success in different endeavors.

Let us share with you some confidence-building habits.

Accept Your Fear Instead of Running Away from It

Fear is nothing but a glitch in your mind. You may think you cannot do something only because you believe that. You cannot embark on new adventures unless you overcome your fears.

To become more confident, you must accept and face your fears head-on instead of running away from them. Here's what you should do:

- Write down what you are frightened of and everything that keeps you from believing in yourself. For instance, if you are scared of wearing pantsuits because you think you'll look hideous, put that on the list. If you want to create your vlog but are afraid of people may make fun of you, jot that down.

- Create a step-by-step plan on how to face and manage that fear. For instance, you could make your vlog by creating short 20-second TikTok videos or videos for other video-based social media platforms. Do this weekly and then share it on other social media.

- Start taking those steps to face your fears.

You can ask your accountability buddy to support you in this time and help you accept your fears. Through the process, give yourself powerful suggestions such as "I can do this," "I am facing my fears head-on," "I accept my fear of (name the fear), and I'm taking active steps to combat it successfully," and the likes.

Communicate Your Needs & Wants Assertively

We often don't get what we want, not because our wants are not correct, but because we don't communicate them effectively. Confidence is about conveying your message, needs, and wants assertively and correctly to your listeners. Be it your team members, coworkers, superiors, family members, friends, or followers, if you want to be the apple of everyone's eye while ensuring they listen to you, you must communicate with them effectively.

- Think of what you wish to communicate to someone before saying it.

- Frame the sentences and the entire talk in your head.

- Filter out any harmful, harsh, and impolite words from the conversation.

- Take care to keep the tone of the sentences clear and direct.

- Before actually saying what you wish to say, greet that person nicely while maintaining direct eye contact.

- Ask the person about their health and life happenings, and then steer the conversation towards the main agenda of the discussion.

- Speak politely and firmly, and detail out all you wish to say.

- Give the other person time to reflect on the talk and reach an informed decision.

- Don't budge from your stance; stick to it assertively.

Follow these guidelines religiously for some time, and very soon, you'll get the hang of communicating your needs and wants assertively to others.

Make Decisions Based on Values, Not Feelings

Many of us are guilty of reacting to situations, and making decisions based on whims and feelings instead of careful thought. The issue also comes from not being clear on your core values and not using them to put your foot down.

Revisit your core values, and detail them to ensure you know them with absolute clarity. Perhaps, your ideals have changed with time, so it is best to take stock of them regularly. Use your core values to make little to big decisions.

Every time you need to decide on something, be it the business model for your new software business or whether or not to shift to a new county, make the call using your core values, not your feelings.

Be Compassionate with Yourself After Mistakes

Being confident is not just about being assertive and strong. It is also about being kind, especially to yourself. Every time you falter and make mistakes — and you will— remember to be nice to yourself. Being kind to yourself gives you the strength to get back after a failed attempt and keep going forward, come what may.

Confidence also comes with and grows better as you build the habit of thinking positively. The next chapter explores habits revolving around positive thinking.

Chapter 23: The Positive Thinking Habits

"Our attitude towards life determines life's attitude towards us." — **John Mitchell**

When life gives us lemons, we usually complain about "the unfairness." At that point, we don't realize that we get what we put out into the universe. Certain unforeseen and unfortunate events in life are outside our control and are more of a test.

However, if you put those events aside and analyze the course and shape of your life, you will realize that your life is the sum of your thoughts, beliefs, attitudes, behaviors, and actions. How our life treats us depends very significantly on our core attitude.

If we focus too much on the negative things in life and all the problems we experience, we only get more of those in return. On the contrary, if we are optimistic and courageous, we start to manifest that positivity in our life too.

It is crucial to mention the universal 'law of attraction' (LOA) here. The law states that "like attracts like," which means if you are positive, you will attract positivity and reap negativity if you are always negative.

To attract only the good things in life, the least you can do is keep a positive mindset. It also plays a magical role in developing your personality.

Let us share some positive thinking habits you can adopt.

Use Positive Words

When speaking and thinking, take great care to use only positive words. Think before speaking, and when you are thinking, actively point out the words with a negative connotation and replace them with positive words.

Eliminate words and suggestions such as, 'I cannot do this, 'can't,' 'don't feel like,' 'incapable of,' 'I am incompetent,' 'miserable,' and other similar words and phrases that constantly highlight issues, weaknesses, and negativity from your thought process and speech.

Take Charge of Your Thoughts

Consciously take charge of your thoughts by tuning into them every hour. Pay attention to what you are thinking about and how that affects your mood, behavior, and actions. If a thought feels unsettling, gently swap it with something more uplifting.

Practice Positive Self-Talk

Your self-talk is the key to nurturing healthy beliefs and thoughts. To start feeling good about yourself, and exude positivity, practice positive self-talk.

- Check-in with your thoughts throughout the day.

- When you notice an unsettling thought, omit the negative and stressful words from it, and swap those with happier and more optimistic replacements.

- Chant that thought a couple of times to help it settle in your head.

- Every time you err, say something uplifting and encouraging to yourself, such as, 'It's okay, let's try again.'

- When you do something well, appreciate your efforts with suggestions such as, 'Good job!' 'Yay! I did it,' and the likes.

In this manner, keep talking politely and kindly to yourself; you'll be amazed at how optimistic you start feeling in a few days.

Show Gratitude

Gratitude is a virtue that makes your heart swell with happiness and live with peace and contentment. It is also a vital ingredient in brewing a positive mind.

Being grateful for your many blessings, including the people around you, boosts your emotional well-being, and when you feel happy, you think happy thoughts.

Here's how you can start showing more gratitude:

- When you wake up, pay your gratitude for anything you feel happy about. It could be the feeling of waking up, having a good night's sleep, waking up next to loved ones, or anything else you feel good about.

- Take a 10-second gratitude break every 2 hours and just reflect on anything you feel thankful for. It could be the food on your table, clothes on your skin, the car you are driving or the bus you are riding, the work you are doing, etc.

- Note down any five things you feel extremely grateful for at the end of the day.

- Throughout the day, make a conscious effort to thank anyone and everyone who assists you in any way.

- Also, show gratitude to yourself for working hard throughout the day and pushing yourself forward irrespective of the obstacles.

It takes consistent effort to practice genuine gratefulness habitually, but once you build this habit, you will only find yourself surrounded by beauty and tranquility.

Read Books that Uplift Your Spirit

Feed your mind some positive mental food by reading books that help you become mentally strong, stable, courageous, optimistic, and confident. Here are some feel-good books that rejuvenate your spirits:

- The Midnight Library by Matt Haig

- Beach Read by Emily Henry

- Redhead by the Side of the Road by Anne Tyler

- Dear Emmie Blue by Lia Louis

Look for books based on your interest, but make sure to find some engaging and light reads that give you a break from the chaos around you.

Think About Things That Move You Closer To Your Goals

During the day, take short breaks to think about your goals and visualize yourself achieving them. If you plan to be a successful digital marketer, think of the kind of digital marketing agency you wish to run, spend some time with digital marketers, and scroll through the pages of successful brands you wish to offer your services.

Similarly, whatever your goal is, think of things relevant to it to draw the goal closer to yourself.

Believe, Believe, and Believe Some More!

Belief is the most powerful emotion there can ever be. When you truly believe you are happy, happy emotions start to bubble inside you. To reap the full power of believing, you need to believe you are successful, confident, and strong.

Create a persona for yourself and all the things you wish to do and imagine yourself in that role. If you want to have a lean, muscular body, drive a Ferrari, and earn a 7-figure income, write that down, and believe you can do it. Once you start truly believing in the power of the universe, you will be amazed at how quickly you start to materialize your deepest and most genuine desires.

Performing Strategy

Go through the different habits you have learned about in this chapter and analyze the following for them. Yes, we have discussed these points before, but what if you just landed on this part.

Duration: Start every habit with a low time interval and gradually build on it. Observe yourself as you engage in the habit in the limited time and make adjustments accordingly.

Best time: Practice gratitude, positive thinking, jogging, and other self-care habits at different times to figure out the most suitable time for each practice.

Important insights: Check how the weather, environment, sleep routine, mood, and other factors affect your performance in every habit. You may perform better under certain circumstances. Once you make those discoveries, you need to incorporate those into your habit routine.

How to Perform: Try the habit in different ways, stacked upon other habits, and experiment with new approaches. This helps you understand every habit's best and most effective performance strategy.

A Strategy to Practice all the Personal Growth Habits together

Here is an example strategy of intertwining the different mindset habits to optimize their effectiveness.

- Go for a quick jog.

- Meditate immediately after your jog.

- Spend 5 minutes thinking of things you love.

- Eat a green fruit or vegetable.

- Have a soothing shower.

- Give yourself a powerful, confidence-based suggestion.

- Talk positively to yourself.

- Think of 3 things you are grateful for in different aspects of your life.

- Imagine yourself living your dream life.

Follow this process step-by-step to fashion a great personal growth routine of your own. Personal growth advances to a whole new level when you infuse time management into the equation. The next part of the book focuses on that.

Part 8: Time Management Habits

"You leave old habits behind by starting out with the thought, 'I release the need for this in my life'."

— **Wayne W. Dyer**

Time Management Habits: Introduction

This part of the book will teach you how getting time management right leads to smart work and efficiency.

Time management is planning and organizing how you allocate your time between different tasks. Almost all the high achievers you have met have probably practiced time management to perfection. Despite getting the same 24 hours we all get, they tend to get more done.

Effective time management is important because it leads to higher productivity and efficiency, which directly helps reduce your stress level. Furthermore, getting your tasks done as early as possible also gives you a better professional reputation, which adds to better chances of promotion and advancement, thus allowing you to achieve more in life and fulfill your career goals.

Mastering the habit of time management allows you to excel at every stage in life, from your childhood to adulthood and beyond, in both your professional and personal relationships.

2 • SCOTT ALLAN

Chapter 24: The Self Discipline Habit

"When a man is sufficiently motivated, discipline will take care of itself." — **Albert Einstein**

In layman's terms, self-discipline is the ability to take action, stay motivated, and push yourself forward regardless of how you feel.

It makes one effectively lead themselves and others in all aspects of life. Self-control and focus, the integral components of self-discipline, are the springs from which happiness, success, and achievement spout.

A lack of self-discipline is one of the core factors that keep us from reaching our greatest potential. This habit is the hardest to develop and hold on to for most people.

To build the self-discipline habit, empower yourself with these healthy habits:

Remove Distractions

Distractions of all forms keep us from achieving our daily targets. A helpful piece of advice is "Out of sight, out of mind." By removing your greatest distraction from sight, for example, your smartphone, you can focus more on the given task.

Countdown, then take action

When feeling extremely demotivated, this trick might come in handy.

Start your countdown from a low number in descending order —for example, from 10 to 1. Force yourself back on the task as soon as your countdown ends, giving yourself a mental push to start working.

Put your goals where you can see them every day

One of the major keys to self-discipline and success is to define clear and specific goals and put your goals in writing where you can see them every day.

Writing goals on a piece of paper that you then put in your wallet, posting them on the fridge, and making your goals a note on your desktop or mobile phone are common ways of looking at your goals daily.

Remind yourself why you started

Mental obstacles like self-doubt and fear can make us go off track and lose focus on our goals.

When you think about quitting, just remind yourself why you started the particular process in the first place. Remind yourself about all the days when you thought you could not move forward due to any problem, but you found a way to overcome that. Use the same motivation and give yourself a push start.

"I'm not telling you it's going to be easy. I'm telling you it's going to be worth it."

Anonymous

Set small goals first

Setting small goals is not the same as breaking significant goals into smaller ones. It means to set small goals, regardless of the large ones ahead.

For example, instead of setting a goal to lose 20kgs in a week, put a small goal of "eating one healthy meal this week." This will help you build the momentum and the confidence to achieve larger goals later.

Practice prioritizing

To practice prioritizing, you must know which tasks are worth putting your most effort into at any given time, then dedicate the most time, effort, and energy to those tasks. Organizing your day based on the job would help you achieve the mission.

In addition, put the tasks you do not necessarily like at the top of your priority list instead of putting them off for another day or two.

Know your weaknesses

Building strong self-discipline demands that you know your weaknesses.

It gives you a better understanding of yourself and how you process as a person. Moreover, it also helps you understand the factors that hold you back and ways to overcome them.

Work on your weaknesses to know how best to combat them and, most importantly, how to prevent them from happening again. At the same time, doing so, practice time management habits to improve your time management abilities.

Chapter 25: The Time Management Habit

*"The bad news is time flies. The good news is you're the pilot."— **Michael Altshuler.***

Time management is critical to get the most out of your day and remaining productive. Time management is about staying focused, changing your behavior for the better, and devoting attention and effort to each task.

Efficient time management will help you improve and progress throughout your career in your professional life. Organizing each day to complete your tasks on time, staying engaged and focused during important meetings, and being creative in your studies are key ways to manage your time well.

Along with our professional life, time management allows us to manage the work-life balance in a perfect ratio without disturbing either of them. Thanks to time management, after leaving the workplace satisfied, it is easier to spend time with our friends and family without being stressed about work.

In contrast, being unable to manage your time correctly will leave you overwhelmed and stressed, along with a tight work schedule that you are behind on.

Below are habits that will help you manage your time exceptionally well.

Set the goals right away

Achieving your goals at the right time is a core part of time management.

When it comes to time management, setting the right goals is crucial. Start with small goals, and that is not breaking larger goals into smaller ones. Setting those small goals will help you achieve them immediately, giving you a head start and motivating you to do more.

Prioritize work

When prioritizing work, it is better to list all your tasks and then prioritize them—set reminders about priority tasks and why you have made them your priority. Use post-it notes to help you with the functions.

Audit your time for seven days straight

Auditing and taking accountability is an excellent way to manage time.

Assess how you spend your time daily and record it. Split the day into hours and analyze where you have worked and where you might have wasted your time. Reduce time wastage and increase work in any deserving area.

By the end of the week, you will have the numbers in the form of working, time-wasting, relaxing, etc., which will make it easier for you to make changes.

Start with your most important task.

Starting with the most critical task increases your productivity because there are fewer distractions and interruptions in the morning.

In addition, we feel more motivated and focused on work early in the morning rather than later in the day. Finishing the critical and challenging tasks would motivate you to do more, and finishing smaller studies later would feel like a reward.

Avoid multitasking

If you want to get more work done in a lesser time, stop multitasking. As good as it sounds, multitasking is an inefficient way of completing your tasks as you will not focus entirely on one charge.

On the other hand, mono-tasking is an efficient and productive way of handling your tasks. Taking one job at a time will have your complete attention and focus, leading you to make fewer mistakes.

Delegate work

Delegating work means handing your workload to someone else and giving them the authority to complete it. This method is available to people in a management-level positions and above.

This time-saving method allows you to hand off some of your workloads to your subordinates and focus on the critical tasks yourself.

Take regular breaks

Taking small and regular breaks allows us to relieve our stress and tension productively.

It allows you to boost your concentration level and increase your focus while working. You also achieve effectiveness and efficiency by taking healthy time short breaks.

However, only engage in planned breaks; unplanned breaks only act as interruptions and distractions from work.

Schedule email response time

Emails are critical and a fast and more convenient way to communicate than phone calls, especially in your professional life. However, opening hundreds of emails daily is no small or easy task.

Set aside time to respond to emails, as managing that poorly will hinder your productivity.

Organize your inbox in different folders, labels, and categories to help you efficiently select and work on emails.

Manage to-do list notes

A to-do list lists all the tasks you need to carry out in the day or week. At the top are the priority tasks, followed by low-priority ones.

By making a to-do list, you ensure you have all your tasks written down in one place and do not forget anything important. You can assess which task needs your immediate attention and which job you can do later.

Once you get the hang of these habits, time management will come naturally to you. Build habits to exercise the 80/20 rule to take things up a notch.

Chapter 26: The 80/20 Habit

"The way to create something great is to create something simple." — **Richard Koch**

As we had mentioned earlier, the 80/20 rule, also called the Pareto rule, states that the relationship between the input you are putting and the output you receive is hardly ever balanced. It says that 20% of your efforts produce 80% of the result.

To make the most effective use of your time, you should learn to recognize and focus on the 20% effort you put in.

If you are skeptical, we understand. Try following the 80/20 rule for a few days and see for yourself!

Identify all your daily/weekly tasks

When it comes to your professional life, identifying and prioritizing your tasks is important, especially when the Pareto rule comes into play.

Use a planner or a to-do list to track your daily tasks; it saves time and is a productive way to keep the record.

Identify key tasks

After identifying your daily/weekly tasks, the next step is to determine which functions out of the list are key tasks. These are the crucial tasks that you must prioritize.

What are the tasks that give you more return?

After successfully identifying the critical tasks, assess the functions that give more return.

In simple terms, you will have to assess and identify which tasks are important enough to get the 20% effort but will produce the 80% output.

Brainstorm how you can reduce or transfer the tasks that give you less return

After selecting the tasks that require your 20% effort for the 80% output, you will see which tasks give you less return. The best way to reduce or transfer those tasks is to delegate them to your subordinates or share them with your coworkers who may help you out in this regard.

Create a plan to do more that brings you more value

Make a plan to do more tasks of great importance in your professional life.

Extremely crucial tasks are beneficial for the business in the long run, and planning on completing those would undoubtedly put you in a good light with the management.

Use 80/20 to prioritize any project you are working on

As a project manager, you want to complete the briefing and start the work as soon as possible.

A lecture of 2 hours would be less efficient than a slideshow or chart spanning over 30 minutes that briefly explain the project and its steps.

Set a plan to focus on activities that bring the most result

Doing exercises that get the most result first is the best way.

Use a planner to write down the tasks guaranteed to help you complete the activity on time. Starting on these tasks as early as possible in the morning is an efficient way to experience enhanced productivity as fewer distractions occur. Another reason this works effectively is that you are more active and energetic in the morning than later in the day.

To keep rocking at time management, build the time blocking habit. We will discuss different micro patterns to help you develop this particular habit.

Chapter 27: Time Blocking Habit

"Out of routine comes inspiration." – **Mike Kostabi**

Time blocking is a crucial productivity technique that involves doing a single high-priority task, or a group of functions, in a specific time "block."

Time blocking allows us to prioritize important tasks with time-sensitive matters, progress on projects, and deal with clients without being available 24 hours a day. These habits help you deal with important tasks and complete them on time.

Adding blocks to your time might sound like messing up your calendar. In contrast, filling up your calendar with important tasks and duties will be difficult for others to distract you.

Develop your list

When you decide to begin time blocking, the first thing to manage is making a list.

List down the things you need to get done for the following week. These include work tasks and activities, family time, every goal you have to achieve for the week, etc.

When it comes to crucial appointments and projects, add a symbol next to it, displaying its importance level, for example, a friend's wedding.

Start with high-level priorities

You have added your tasks and activities to the list for the day/week.

Knowing your high-level priorities is essential here as you will shape your schedule around those activities. Starting early in the morning is a good time as there are fewer distractions, and you are completely active and energetic.

Try to limit your top priority tasks to 2-3 per day for your ease

Create a daily blueprint

While making a blueprint, you must assess how much time you have in the day and how much you can assign to each task.

Depending on the job, the blueprint should account for daily tasks, meetings, short breaks, traveling, and client meetings.

The main focus, however, is on your important tasks and projects.

Set aside time for both deep and shallow work

Deep work is long-term work such as writing, coding, and designing where you want to work without distractions. You must set aside huge blocks of time specifically for this purpose

On the other hand, shallow work is short-term work such as phone calls and email responses, also known as reactive tasks.

Add blocks for reactive tasks each day

Regarding reactive tasks, add blocks for them, despite how small they seem. Be realistic about the time reactive tasks may take before dedicating a time block to them.

Write down your daily to-do list

Ensure you down your tasks for the upcoming day and put them in the appropriate times. Ensure you have ample slots for both shallow and deep tasks.

You must remember that this is just a framework of how it should work. It might take you some time to get the to-do list right.

Having discussed the different habits, let us examine their performance strategy.

Performing Strategy

Duration: Decide a specific time duration for every habit and religiously stick to it. Begin working on a habit for a couple of minutes, then gradually increase the duration.

Best time: Work on a respective habit at different times: morning, noon, afternoon, evening, and night. If you wake up at dawn, try a habit at that time. This practice helps you identify the most profitable time for the habit, allowing you to leverage it to the maximum.

Important Insights: Pay attention to how environmental factors, behavioral factors, sleep routine, diet and hydration levels, and other elements affect your engagement and performance in a habit.

How to Perform: There can be multiple ways to do the same thing. You can write your daily to-do list on an actual notepad or the tablet on your phone or computer.

You can use a scheduling app to schedule emails or delegate tasks to your subordinate. You can play your goals right away or do it the night before. The point is that there is no one specific way to perform a certain practice. You must try different things to understand and develop the best approach to delivering a high-performance outcome.

A Strategy to Practice all the Time Management Habits Together

Here is a helpful strategy that can help you combine the different time management habits discussed above to make the most of them as one habit stack.

- Set your goals right away.

- Note down your goals and put them where you can see them.

- Think of the reasons why you need to achieve your targets.

- Begin with the most critical task.

- Work on one task at a time.

- Delegate specific tasks to people better equipped to handle them.

- Schedule your email response time.

- Work on tasks following the 80/20 rule.

- Work on deep and shallow tasks

- Time block your different activities

Try your hand at this routine. Like the other habits, you can also set reminders for this one. It takes a couple of days to settle into the practice, but you will see a rapid boost in your productivity once you get the hang of it.

While working on improving our health, happiness, mindset, time management, productivity, fitness, and other aspects of our lives, we sometimes forget an integral area: our spirituality.

Life only becomes more meaningful when you have a clear sense of identity and purpose. That's what your spirituality is all about. You may not truly comprehend its importance until you start working on unlocking it for real.

Let us discuss some powerful spiritual habits in the following part of the book.

Part 9: Spirituality Habits

"Humans are imperfect creatures. You don't 'succeed' because you have no weaknesses; you succeed because you find your unique strengths and focus on developing habits around them."

— **Tim Ferriss**

Spirituality Goals: Introduction

We face different troubles, insecurities, fears, losses, and grief in our lives from time to time. These occurrences affect our mental health, and we may fall victim to depression and anxiety. However, when we connect to our spiritual side, we find it easy to overcome these troubles because we know our purpose in life.

Having a clear sense of purpose and direction to follow resolves many issues. When we know what we want and where we are heading, we find the strength to battle our griefs, doubts, fears, and challenges.

This part of the book will introduce you to spiritual habits and how to inculcate these to bring a better change in your life.

Spirituality nurtures inner peace and growth. Once you build some powerful spiritual habits, they become a source of harmony and hope for you. Consequently, these habits grant you contentment and make you a better person.

If you wish to rejuvenate your soul, understand and build the spiritual habits presented in this section.

Chapter 28: The Gratitude Habit

"The chains of habit are too weak to be felt until they are too strong to be broken." **– Samuel Johnson**

The first step toward spirituality is to grow the attitude of gratitude in your daily life. Most often focus on what we desire rather than what we already have. If we try to be aware of our countless blessings, we can easily find moments of gratitude in our everyday life.

No matter how hard life is on you, find in yourself the graciousness to feel blessed for the food on your table, your house, and your job. Many people in this world do not have access to these necessities. Most of all, be thankful for this life which is a gift.

Once you cultivate the habit of gratitude, you will see how it will transform your state of mind and your life outlook. You will have the power to turn problems into possibilities and impatience into calmness. The real challenge is to train yourself to master this skill so well that it becomes second nature to you.

This chapter will teach you micro habits that will help you do that:

Start Small

When you start something new, you don't have to start big. Lao Tzu rightly said that the journey of a thousand miles begins with a single step. Gratitude is incredibly simple. You can start by taking five minutes out of your busy routine to appreciate something good that happened to you. It can be time spent with a friend, something pleasant someone said, or a meal you liked that day.

Stop comparing, right NOW

If you sincerely want to master the gratitude habit, comparing yourself to other people is a big NO. It is very tempting to compare your life to other people's, especially in this age of social media, but doing so will do you no good.

Learn to appreciate yourself and celebrate with others. A smart strategy is to note down three things you find good about yourself that you can identify as your strengths. Another way is to limit the use of social media because everything you see on social media is not valid.

Get your friends and family involved

You can get help from your friends and family to practice gratitude consistently. Make it a habit to have everyone mention their grateful moment from the day before every meal. If someone forgets, others can act as reminders. Doing this will strengthen the practice and let everyone experience gratitude. After this brief moment of appreciation, you will feel a shift in the energy in the room.

Remember to do it

The most challenging part of adopting any new habit is remembering to do it daily. You can make gratitude a part of your daily routine by indulging in a brief moment of gratitude immediately after waking up in the morning or before going to bed at night. Writing it in your journal will also help you build consistency.

Don't forget to rewire

It is natural to get involved in your routine tasks after expressing gratitude in one instance. But you must give yourself enough time to absorb this by dedicating a few seconds after every such episode. Follow every gratitude moment with fifteen seconds of silence to relish the experience.

Find a cue that works for you

Triggers play an essential role in building new habits in your lifestyle. You can use the idea of habit stacking to stick with the gratitude habit —but use any cue that works for you. Practicing the gratitude habit with a meal is a good option because it helps you share your gratitude practice with others.

Go deeper

After successfully expressing gratitude for a few days, you must dive deeper to explore other benefits of gratitude. You can build more sophisticated cues such as phone calls. Whenever you get a call, take a moment to appreciate your relations and then answer the call. Practicing this regularly will help you experience each phone conversation with a deep sense of gratitude.

Keep it regular

As important as building new habits is, it is equally important to sustain them. Consistency is the key to growing a mindset of gratitude and making it a part of your lifestyle.

You can do this by looking around to find the best things and engaging in mini-moments of gratitude. Be focused on your gratitude goals and replenish your soul by sharing positive energies with the people around you.

Chapter 29: The Smiling Habit

Happiness is a habit—cultivate it. — **Elbert Hubbard**

A smile is a powerful tool to connect with others and feel good about yourself and your life. Several studies have found that smiling has a profound impact on your well-being. If you commit to smiling more often, you will start living a happier life.

Researchers believe that a smile stimulates a particular set of muscles in the face —muscles strongly associated with feelings of happiness and joyfulness. When you smile, you send signals to the emotional center of your mind to indicate that all is well. This reduces stress and increases contentment.

Shawn Achor says adopting smiling as a regular habit has multiple benefits, such as lifting your mood and raising your emotional intelligence level. Although small seeming, this change can be contagious. And the best thing about a smile is that it is free.

This chapter offers practical tips to make smiling a permanent habit in your life.

Practice Smiling

Smile right now, no matter where you are reading this. Put a big smile on your face and try to imagine something negative in your mind. You won't manage to do it because it is hard to hold any unhappy feelings while smiling.

You can start by smiling three times extra in a day in addition to your usual smiles. This should include situations when you do not smile normally, such as formal meet-ups or official presentations. You can do this for an entire week—consider it a seven-day smiling trial. Remind yourself to smile periodically throughout the day, even if you have to force it.

You can eventually develop smiling as a habit by following a few simple tips.

- Place visible notes with a smiley face image in your home and office to remind yourself to smile often.

- Set plenty of reminders on your phone to prompt you to smile every few hours.

- Mark entries in your calendar every time you smile.

- Smile in front of a mirror and notice your facial expressions. Keep this impression in your mind to recreate that moment whenever you see someone.

- Smile the instant you get up in the morning. Go to bed with a smile on your face.

Give Yourself a Smile Cue

Now that you have learned the importance of a smile and how to practice it, remember to do it as you go through your day. The trick is to create some cues and smile every time you encounter these cues for one week.

Some ideal cues are:

- A sound you often hear during a day, for example, your ringtone or an email alert beep.

- Any action can make you remember to smile, such as sitting in or getting out of your car or holding the door handle when you enter your home or office.

- A visual sign, like seeing someone having coffee or watching someone smiling

Stay Motivated

Motivation is the key to building new habits. You can motivate yourself to smile by keeping in mind its benefits. Remember that you like the people who smile while they talk to you. They create a pleasant impression as it makes them look confident and welcoming.

Smiling on the phone will soften your speaking tone, enabling you to build a better connection with the listener. Another way to motivate yourself is to write down a commitment like, "This week, I will smile every time I think of or encounter my smile cue."

Smiling more is a quick and easy way to improve your quality of life. It does not require any significant effort on your part. You only have to stick to a smile, and you will be more contented.

Chapter 30: The Journaling Habit

"Do the best you can, until you know better. Then when you know better, do better." — **Maya Angelou**

A great way to connect with your soul is to express your thoughts and feelings in a journal. It would help if you adopted it as a spiritual habit as it offers countless benefits that remain true in your life.

Firstly, journaling helps you be more productive by focusing on specific goals and tasks. You learn to live in the present and become more mindful as a person. Journaling improves your memory and boosts your emotional intelligence. It also reduces stress and enhances your mental well-being.

Human memory fades with time and becomes vague with age. When you keep a journal, you record your memories, past experiences, and life lessons that can shape your future.

It is hard to build new habits; that's why we are making an effort in this book to encourage you to write in a personal journal every day. You will learn how to do it and make it an essential part of your daily life.

Set Aside Time Daily

You have to make a strict commitment to yourself to schedule time for journaling. Set aside five, ten, or twenty minutes daily for this activity. It can be any time convenient for you. Ideally, it should be morning as your mind is most active at that time. If your mornings are busy, you can choose nighttime to document everything that happened that day.

Use the Right Journaling Tools

Choosing the proper journaling method and tools is the key to building consistency in your habit. Start with a handwritten journal first, as it is easy to maintain. A digital journal is another option you may utilize. There are also different mobile applications that make journaling quite enjoyable. Try each tool for a few days, then commit to the one you find more compelling.

Create the right journaling environment

You have to create a comfortable environment for journaling with no noise and distractions. Since you write about yourself and your thoughts, you need isolation in a place or room far from others' presence. Technology is also a big distraction in the current era; avoid its use while journaling.

Protect your Privacy

You should protect the privacy of your journal at any cost. The simplest way is to carry it in your bag at all times. That way, you will have your journal if you feel an unexpected situation where you need to write down your thoughts immediately. Do not allow anyone to have a look at your journal, no matter how much you trust that person.

Date Each Entry

You must make entries in your journal with the exact date and time. Dating is important because you may be urged to look back at your journal entries later. Dated entries can help you understand the thought process behind important life events.

What to Write in Your Personal Journal?

Before adopting this as a habit, you must know what to write in your journal. There are quite a few different types of journaling. You have to find what suits you best and fulfill your aims of journaling.

For example, you can write down the three things you're most grateful for, your most important goal for the day, and lessons you learned from the previous day. Studies have shown that writing about harrowing life experiences releases stress and improves physical and mental health.

Be Honest with Yourself

Journal is something you are writing for yourself; therefore, you can be honest and genuine. You should sound authentic and reflect on your original thoughts. Do not hesitate to write about something that bothered you. Be open about your emotions and record how you feel instead of thinking about how you should feel.

Focus on Simplicity

You do not have to buy fancy notebooks or expensive journals. You can start journaling from a simple lined notebook. Also, remember that journaling is not a professional piece of writing. You do not have to worry about language or grammar. If you care too much about formalities, you will require more time to transfer your thoughts on paper. The whole activity will feel like a monotonous task instead of a therapeutic exercise.

It is a matter of time until journaling moves to your autopilot mode. That's when you find a natural inclination to practice and enjoy doing it too.

Let us now move to the performing strategy of spirituality habits.

Performing Strategy

Duration: Set a fixed time for each spirituality habit and observe it strictly for some days. If you plan to journal, start with 5 minutes, and stick to it. After a few weeks, stretch the time.

Best time: Try each habit at different times. You can only know the best time to work on a practice when you have tried it at other times. Perhaps, you can journal better at night and enjoy practicing gratitude early in the day. Experimenting is the only way to get this understanding.

Important insights: Watch yourself closely when working on different habits, and see how your mood, sleep, health, environment, and other factors affect a particular habit.

Perhaps you don't have the strength to smile or be grateful when you have only slept for 3 hours, but you feel thankful and happy when you have slept for 8 hours. Such insights help you know what factors to improve to get the most out of a habit.

How to Perform: Like figuring out the best time to work on a habit, figure out the most suitable performing strategy by trying different ways to work on a particular habit.

A Strategy to Practice all the Mindset Habits together

Here's a simple strategy you can try to bring all the mindset habits together.

- Begin your day by smiling.

- When you smile, think of anything you feel grateful for at that moment or in life.

- During the day, be kind to everyone, and control the urge to compare yourself to anyone.

- Write down any one thing you are wondering about a lot or contemplate your purpose in life, and write down the findings in your journal.

- Carry on with this same cycle 2 to 3 times during the day.

Make a mission to start working on these practices and give yourself a couple weeks to stay consistent.

A Simple Conclusion

Changing the course of your life for the better is not impossible. Yes, it takes a bit of hard work, but if you do that smartly, even that is not an uphill task. The many success habits I have shared with you, all broken down into micro habits, are perfect for shaping your life into a thriving one.

I wish you all the best as you work to create a happy, prosperous future, and I am ever so grateful to you for taking the time to read this book. It is a life-changer, but only if you let it be. I know for sure you will only make the right decision for yourself!

"If you pick the right small behavior and sequence it right, then you won't have to motivate yourself to have it grow. It will just happen naturally, like a good seed planted in a good spot." – BJ Fogg

About Scott Allan

Scott Allan is an international bestselling author of 25+ books published in 7 languages in personal growth and self-development. He is the author of **Fail Big, Undefeated,** and **Do the Hard Things First.**

As a former corporate business trainer in Japan and **Transformational Mindset Strategist,** Scott has invested over 10,000 hours of research and instructional coaching into self-mastery and leadership training.

Scott Allan is committed to a path of constant and never-ending self-improvement with an unrelenting passion for teaching, building critical life skills, and inspiring people worldwide to take charge of their lives.

Many success strategies and self-empowerment material reinventing lives worldwide evolve from Scott Allan's 20 years of practice and teaching critical skills to corporate executives, individuals, and business owners.

You can connect with Scott at:

scottallan@scottallanpublishing.com

Visit author. to/ScottAllanBooks to stay up to date on future book releases.

Books Change Lives.
Let's Change Yours Today.

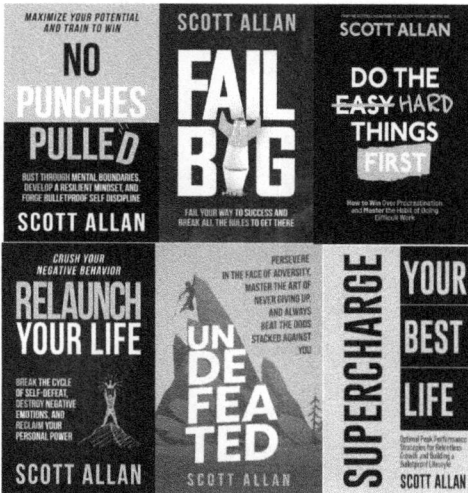

Scott Allan

"Master Your Life One Book at a Time."

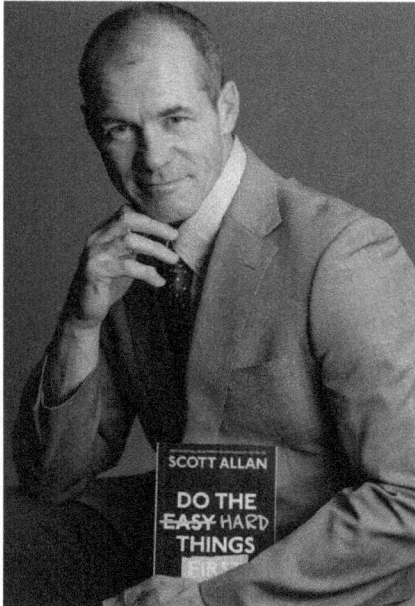

<u>Subscribe</u> to the weekly newsletter for actionable content and updates on future book releases from Scott Allan

Scott Allan
P U B L I S H I N G
MASTER YOUR LIFE **ONE BOOK AT A TIME**

S A